Class Management in the Secondary School

Successful secondary teachers operate in many different ways but they have one thing in common – an ability to manage their classrooms effectively. Without the skills required to do this, the most inspiring and knowledgeable teacher will fail.

In *Class Management in the Secondary School*, Ted Wragg helps teachers to clarify their own aims and to find the strategies which will work for them. Topics covered include:

- first encounters
- establishing rules and relationships
- managing time and space
- coping with specific discipline problems

There are certain skills that teachers possess that are of paramount importance and class management is one of those areas in which teachers need to be strong in order to do their job effectively. Class management can be the single most influential factor in getting it right and is a core teaching skill that both trainee and experienced teachers should constantly be improving.

Ted Wragg is Professor of Education at Exeter University and the author of over 40 books. He has directed numerous research projects, analysed hundreds of lessons and writes a regular column for the *Times Educational Supplement*.

Successful Teaching Series

This set of practical resource books for teachers focuses on the classroom. The first editions were best sellers and these new editions will be equally welcomed by teachers eager to improve their teaching skills. Each book contains:

- practical, written and oral activities for individual and group use at all stages of professional development
- transcripts of classroom conversation and teacher feedback and photographs of classroom practice to stimulate discussion
- succinct and practical explanatory text

Titles in the *Successful Teaching Series* are

Class Management in the Primary School
E. C. Wragg

Class Management in the Secondary School
E. C. Wragg

Assessment and Learning in the Primary School
E. C. Wragg

Assessment and Learning in the Secondary School
E. C. Wragg

Explaining in the Primary School
E. C. Wragg and G. Brown

Explaining in the Secondary School
E. C. Wragg and G. Brown

Questioning in the Primary School
E. C. Wragg and G. Brown

Questioning in the Secondary School
E. C. Wragg and G. Brown

The first editions were published in the *Leverhulme Primary Project Classroom Skills Series*.

Class Management in the Secondary School

E. C. Wragg

London and New York

First published as *Class Management* in 1993
by Routledge
This new revised edition first published 2001
byRoutledgeFalmer
11 New Fetter Lane, London EC4P 4EE

Simultaneously published in the USA and Canada
by RoutledgeFalmer
29 West 35th Street, New York, NY 10001

RoutledgeFalmer is an imprint of the Taylor & Francis Group

© 2001 E. C. Wragg

Typeset in Palatino by Bookcraft Ltd, Stroud, Gloucestershire
Printed and bound in Great Britain by Bell & Bain Ltd, Glasgow

British Library Cataloguing in Publication Data
A catalogue record for this book is available from the British Library

Library of Congress Cataloging in Publication Data
Wragg, E. C. (Edward Conrad)
    Class management in the seccondary school / E. C. Wragg.
        p. cm. – (Successful teaching series)
    "First published as Class management, 1993" – T.p. verso
    Includes bibliographical references.
    1. Classroom management. 2. High school teaching. I. Wragg,
    E. C. (Edward Conrad). Class management. II. Title. III.
    Successful teaching series (London, England)

LB3013. W74 2001
372.1102'4–dc21   00–051797

ISBN 0–415–24954–6

Contents

Preface

Improving the quality of learning in secondary schools, and preparing children for what will probably be a long and complex life in the twenty-first century, requires the highest quality of teaching and professional training. The *Successful Teaching Series* focuses on the essence of classroom competence, on those professional skills that make a real difference to children, such as the ability to explain clearly, to ask intelligent and thought-provoking questions, to manage classes effectively and to use the assessment of progress to enhance pupils' learning.

'Success' may be defined in many ways. For some it is seen purely in test scores, for others it is a broader issue, involving the whole child. In this series we report what teachers have done that has been judged to be successful or unsuccessful. To do this several criteria have been used: headteachers' assessments, pupil progress measures, esteem from fellow teachers or from children. Skilful teachers ensure that their classes learn something worthwhile; unskilful teachers may turn off that delicate trip-switch in children's psyche which keeps their minds open to lifelong learning.

Experienced teachers engage in hundreds of exchanges every single day of their career, thousands in a year, millions over a professional lifetime. Teaching consists of dozens of favoured strategies that become embedded in deep structures, for there is no time to re-think every single move in a busy classroom. Many decisions are made by teachers in less than a second, so once these *deep structures* have been laid down they are not always amenable to change, even if a school has a well-developed professional development programme. Reflecting on practice alone or with colleagues does enable teachers to think about what they do away from the immediate pressures of rapid interaction and speedy change.

Rejecting the notion that there is only one way to teach, this series of books explores some of the many strategies available to teachers, as well as the patterns of classroom organisation which best assist pupil learning. It demonstrates that teachers, even when working to predetermined work schemes and curricula, must forge their own ways of teaching in the light of the context in which they operate and the evidence available to them from different sources. The series is rooted in classroom observation research over several decades and is designed to assist teachers at all stages of their professional development.

The series also contains an element that is unusual in most of the books that are aimed at helping teachers. Some of the activities assume that teaching should not just be something that teachers do *to* their pupils, but rather *with* them, so the exercises involve teachers and their classes working together to improve teaching and learning; pupils acting as partners, not merely as passive recipients of professional wizardry. Thus the books on class management consider such matters as self-discipline; those on questioning and explaining look at pupils interacting with each other; those on assessment address how children can learn from being assessed and also how they can appraise their own work. When children become adults they will have to be able to act autonomously, so it is crucial that they learn early to take more and more responsibility for their own progress.

The books are useful for:

- practising teachers;
- student teachers;
- college and university tutors, local and national inspectors and advisers;
- school-based in-service co-ordinators, advisory teachers;
- school mentors, appraisers and headteachers.

Like the others in the series, this book can be used as part of initial or in-service programmes in school. Individuals can use it as a source of ideas, and it is helpful in teacher appraisal, in developing professional awareness both for those being appraised and for their appraisers. The suggested activities have been tried out extensively by experienced teachers and those in pre-service training and have been revised in the light of their comments.

The series will provoke discussion, help teachers reflect on their current and future practice and encourage them to look behind, and ask questions about, everyday classroom events.

Acknowledgements

My thanks to the many members of my research teams, especially Gill Haynes, Caroline Wragg, Rosemary Chamberlin, Felicity Wikeley, Kay Wood, Sarah Crowhurst, Clive Carré, Trevor Kerry, Pauline Dooley, Allyson Trotter and Barbara Janssen. Between them, they have observed over two thousand lessons and interviewed teachers, pupils, parents and classroom assistants in hundreds of primary and secondary schools.

I should also like to express my gratitude to the many teachers who teach successfully on a daily basis. A number of the teachers shown at work in the books in the *Successful Teaching Series* are recipients of Platos, which are given to the national winners at the annual Teaching Awards ceremony.

The photographs in this book were taken by Fred Jarvis and Ted Wragg. The cartoons are by Jonathan Hall.

Aims and content

For many years researchers and teachers themselves have tried to find the secrets of successful teaching. The difficulty is that, although there are certain factors which recur over and over again, there can be considerable variations in the local context in which expert teachers work. One skilled practitioner may reward good work from a pupil by praising it, another by displaying it on the wall, a third by giving a written commendation in a record book. Someone else might use a combination of these strategies, or devise yet another.

There are certain skills that teachers possess, like class management, which are of paramount importance. Without the ability to manage a group effectively, any other qualities teachers have may be neutralised. It is no good knowing your subject matter, being able to devise interesting activities appropriate to the topic, knowing what sort of questions to ask or being able to give a clear explanation, if you cannot obtain a hearing or organise a group of children. When three American investigators, Wang, Haertel and Walberg (1993), reviewed hundreds of studies of the many school and policy influences on pupil learning, they reached the conclusion that classroom management was the single most influential factor.

The principal aim of this book, therefore, is to give newcomers to the profession some basic notions and precepts about class management, and also to enable experienced teachers to examine their own practice and, it is hoped, improve it. One of the most satisfying features of teaching is that it is possible to work at and improve one's professional skills throughout one's teaching career. The ideas in the six units are in part based on our own research into classrooms, as well as that of others, and the activities have been tried out and evaluated over several years.

The intention is that, by reading the text and trying out some of the practical activities, teachers will be able to improve their own classroom practice. The emphasis is on both activity and reflection, for one without the other would be less effective. All the activities can be done by individuals or by groups of student or experienced teachers, either in discussion or with children on their own or in someone else's classroom. The use of jargon is minimised, though not omitted entirely. For example, Jacob Kounin's use of terms such as 'withitness' (meaning 'having eyes in the back of your head' or being aware of what is going on in various parts of the classroom) is kept, as these are graphic terms that can easily be remembered.

The book is organised in to the following six units.

In **Unit 1** there is an analysis of what constitutes effective class management.

Unit 2 describes and explores the different philosophies and approaches to class management.

Unit 3 explores the very first encounters that teachers have with a new class.

Unit 4 deals with the two Rs, rules and relationships.

Unit 5 concentrates on decision-making, including the handling of disruptive behaviour.

Unit 6 looks ahead to the development of greater competence in class management.

There is therefore no favouring of a single approach to class management. The emphasis is on teachers exploring the issues, considering alternatives, trying out ideas and then finding their own best way forward in the light of their own experience and that of others.

HOW TO USE THIS BOOK

The six units constitute substantial course material in class management. The activities and text are suitable for in-service and professional studies courses as well as for individual use.

The text may be read as a book in its own right; all the *activities* can be undertaken either by individual teachers or by members of a group working together on the topic.

The discussion activities can be used in group meetings, for example, or as part of staff discussion during a school's INSET day. The individual reader can use these as a prompt for reflection and planning.

The written activities are intended to be worked on individually, but also lend themselves to group discussion when completed.

The practical activities are designed to be done in the teacher's own classroom or by student teachers on teaching practice or when they are teaching children brought into the training institution for professional work.

The book can either be used alone or in conjunction with other books in the *Successful Teaching Series*. Those responsible for courses, therefore, may well wish to put together exercises and activities from several of the books in this series to make up their own course as part of a general professional skills development programme, either in initial training or of whole school professional development. Usually the discussion and written activities described will occupy between an hour and ninety minutes and classroom activities completed in about an hour, though this may vary, depending on the context.

Many of the issues covered in this book are generic and apply to both primary and secondary teaching. Most of the illustrations and examples cited are from the appropriate phase of schooling, but in certain cases they are taken from another year group, either for the sake of clarity, or because the original research work referred to was done with that particular age cohort of pupils.

Unit 1   Skilful class management

The word 'management' is usually associated with the most senior people in an organisation. Ordinary employees are supposed to carry out the daily business, while their better paid superiors 'manage' them. Such managers may live in a remote office, eat in an executive dining room, while avoiding soiling their hands on machine oil and grease.

Teaching is different from that time-honoured stereotype, because even newly qualified teachers have a lot to 'manage'. From the beginning to the end of their careers, teachers are responsible for managing, among other things:

- resources and materials (including quite expensive equipment, in some cases);
- time and space (lesson beginning and end, time spent on activities, layout of room);
- teaching and learning strategies (e.g. use whole class, small groups, individual learning);
- pupils' behaviour, safety and wellbeing, interactions with others, progress;
- relationships in and out of school, including with parents, support staff, other agencies.

If ever you watch young children playing together at home or in school, before long someone will suggest playing at 'school'. At the beginning of this familiar fantasy game a common ritual is followed. One child will step forward and say, 'I'll be the teacher', and from then onwards that person is assumed to be in charge. There is not usually a rush to say, 'Can I be the rather quiet child who sits in a corner getting on obediently with some maths problems', but then children are not prone to use adult language in these matters.

It is fascinating to see what happens next. Most children role-playing as a teacher will immediately move centre stage and start ordering everyone else around, 'Right, you sit here, you go over there.' It seems to be the element of control that attracts. Others mimic a more kindly style. In this mirror of class-room life, where the players know the daily reality better than anyone else, some children will start to misbehave and then may be told off or even some-times whacked about the body or head in a way that would have a real teacher up before the nearest magistrate.

Control over the behaviour of others, however, is only one of the aspects of class management highlighted above. Every day, busy teachers will find they are planning lessons; choosing topics or tasks; making judgements about what they as teachers should determine and what children should be encouraged to decide or choose for themselves; supervising movement around the classroom or school; organising a variety of activities undertaken by individuals, small groups or the whole class; praising good work or reprimanding pupils who misbehave; making sure the right materials and books are available; selecting from a range of possible teaching strategies.

The importance of effective class management is well illustrated by the follow-ing true story. A few years ago I was an external examiner at a college in London. This involved visiting students on teaching practice, seeing them teach and dis-cussing with their tutors and supervising teachers in the schools whether they should pass or fail. I arrived at a school and was met by the head. She told me that the student had had considerable discipline problems, had not been able to control one or two of the more difficult pupils and, in her view, should not be allowed to pass. I watched the student concerned and was surprised at how orderly the class actually was. The lesson was quite interesting, pupils got on with their work and there did not seem to be too much difference between this student and others who were in the lower band of the pass category.

The sequel, however, is interesting. When I spoke to the student, she confessed her surprise at the good behaviour of the class and the relative smoothness of the lesson. Her teaching practice had gone very badly, she explained, because of poor behaviour by the pupils, and she fully expected to fail the course. Indeed, this was the first lesson for weeks that had gone according to plan and in a civilised manner. When I explained to the head what had happened she could not at first believe it. Suddenly she had an idea. 'Let me talk to Jane,' she said.

Five minutes later she returned and all became clear. Jane was the kind-hearted deputy head who normally taught the student's class. Hearing that an external heavy was coming in to assess the student, Jane had gone to the chil-dren and told them that, for once in their lives, they should behave themselves, as Miss X's career was on the line. Children who would walk ten miles to feed a poorly pigeon, but not hesitate to torment a nervous student teacher, had done as she had asked. It seemed a pity that a student, who, with the help of a superordinate external authority in the form of an experienced deputy head, could teach with a modest degree of effectiveness, should be so ineffective on her own. It also confirmed that the ability to control behaviour, in whatever manner, is a 'threshold' measure – if you have enough of it you are over the threshold and can display the rest of your repertoire of professional skills, but too little of it and these may never become apparent.

Life in schools in the twenty-first century is much more demanding than in former times. Awareness of possible unemployment, the demands for greater knowledge and skill, as well as the speed of change, have all exerted greater pressure on teachers during the years of compulsory schooling (Wragg, 1997). The importance attached to results in public examinations, the use of league tables and other means of comparison between primary schools, high profile inspections, close attention from print and broadcast mass media and the prominence given to education by politicians, have produced a system of high accountability. Teachers are under constant scrutiny and are expected to be able to manage their classes effectively.

In the nineteenth century, there were fewer demands and teacher-training institutions were known as 'normal' schools. The assumption was that there was an agreed 'norm', some single approved way of teaching that all must copy. It led to Charles Dickens describing M'Choakumchild in *Hard Times* as like 'some one hundred and forty schoolmasters [who] had been turned at the same time at the same factory, on the same principles, like so many pianoforte legs.'

There have been two contrasting tendencies in the late twentieth and early twenty-first centuries. One has been for more prescription. As was the case with the normal schools, some people advocate conformity to a single prescribed pattern, the most notable form of which was the literacy and numeracy hours imposed in English primary schools in the late 1990s, when the nature of activity every few minutes was centrally determined. The second has been more plural: to encourage a variety of approaches to teaching generally and to class management in particular.

The inability to manage classes skilfully is often the single most common reason for failure on teaching practice and for failing the probationary period. Fear of being unable to control a class is often the greatest anxiety of student teachers before teaching practice (Wragg, 1989). The management of people, time and resources is right at the centre of human skill in a variety of occupations, not just teaching. Those who waste resources, fritter away time or alienate their workmates or their customers are often a source of intense irritation.

In a large-scale study of several hundred teachers alleged to be incompetent (Wragg *et al.*, 2000), we found that fellow teachers were often the most critical group of those teachers who were regarded as incompetent, feeling that one person's ineptitude brought shame on their department or on the whole school staff. In teaching, the ability to use time skilfully, to win the support of children and to make effective use of what are often scarce resources lies at the heart of competence. Time devoted to improving class management is time well spent.

I shall, therefore, adopt the following two principles in what follows:

1   Class management is what teachers do to ensure that children engage in the task in hand, whatever that may be.
2   There are many different ways of achieving the state where children work at the task in hand.

In order to help clarify your own or your colleagues' views of what constitutes effective class management, the following exercise can be undertaken. It is based on, though not identical to, techniques developed in personal construct theory (Kelly, 1970), which allows people to examine their own thinking and constructions by comparing and contrasting individuals and concepts.

Activity 1

Step 1   Think of two teachers who taught you when you were a pupil in primary school (or else of two teachers whose teaching you know well). The first teacher (Teacher A) should be someone in whose lessons you felt pupils learned a lot and enjoyed the class. The second teacher (Teacher B) should be a different teacher, one in whose lessons you felt little was learned and which pupils did not seem to enjoy. To refresh your memory, picture Teacher A and Teacher B as clearly as you can in your mind's eye. Without exaggerating, write a brief descriptive paragraph about each in the spaces provided on the next page or on a separate sheet. These may be quite ordinary things that stick in your mind, such as, 'This teacher always had the patience to explain things clearly to you, even if you did not understand first time. I remember feeling really frustrated about a maths problem once, and she just sat and did it with me until I understood the principle'; or, 'This teacher was sometimes unfair in her use of punishments. Once she kept the whole class in at lunchtime just because one boy had knocked someone's PE kit over, and everyone deeply resented it.'

Step 2   Look at your descriptions and assemble a set of dimensions, using adjectives and phrases that are the opposite of each other like 'tidy – untidy' or 'turned up on time – was often late'. It is not essential that Teachers A and B should be the exact opposite of each other on each dimension: for example, they might both have been strict or neither might have been. It is important that you pick out aspects of teaching *in your own way*, especially where class management is involved, and write these down in your own words. For example, your first four pairs might be:

1 Is strict	Lets children do what they like
2 Has a sense of humour	Has no sense of humour
3 Is businesslike	Is slipshod
4 Interested in individuals	Not interested in individuals

Write up to ten pairs of opposites in the grid below:

1	
2	
3	
4	
5	
6	
7	
8	
9	
10	

TEACHER A

General description

Memorable event 1

Memorable event 2

TEACHER B

General description

Memorable event 1

Memorable event 2

Step 3   Now think of the 'ideal teacher', someone who is supreme at working with children. This person might be similar to Teacher A, but not necessarily so, since no one is perfect. You should attempt to define what, for you, is the ideal teacher on a seven-point scale, using your own list of ten pairs of opposites. For example, suppose you think that your ideal teacher would be slightly strict, have a good sense of humour, be pretty businesslike and be very interested in individuals, then your grid might look like the example below.

1 Is strict	1 2 ③ 4 5 6 7	Lets children do what they like
2 Has a sense of humour	1 ② 3 4 5 6 7	Has no sense of humour
3 Is businesslike	1 ② 3 4 5 6 7	Is slipshod
4 Interested in individuals	① 2 3 4 5 6 7	Not interested in individuals

Now write your own pairs of opposites in the grid below and rate the ideal teacher by circling the appropriate number on each seven-point scale.

1	1 2 3 4 5 6 7	
2	1 2 3 4 5 6 7	
3	1 2 3 4 5 6 7	
4	1 2 3 4 5 6 7	
5	1 2 3 4 5 6 7	
6	1 2 3 4 5 6 7	
7	1 2 3 4 5 6 7	
8	1 2 3 4 5 6 7	
9	1 2 3 4 5 6 7	
10	1 2 3 4 5 6 7	

Step 4   The next stage is to think once more about these attributes, but this time to give an honest appraisal of yourself, either as you think you are, if you are already teaching, or as you think you will be when you start. With the thought *'myself'* put a *cross* through the appropriate number on the seven-point scales above. You should do this as honestly as you can, being neither too severe nor too generous with yourself. When you have finished, you can compare your self-appraisal with your own ideal. For example, if you saw yourself as fairly permissive, with a bit of a sense of humour, slightly slipshod and interested in individuals, then your grid would look something like the grid on the next page.

This would show that you are close to what you perceive to be the ideal teacher on two of your dimensions – humour and interest in individuals – but some distance away on strictness and being businesslike. The benefit of this analysis is not that it tells you exactly what kind of person you really are (you would need comments from other people to have a better idea of that), but that it allows you to compare yourself with your ideal on your own set of criteria.

1 Is strict	1 2 ③ 4 5 ⑥ 7	Lets children do what they like
2 Has a sense of humour	1 ② ⑶ 4 5 6 7	Has no sense of humour
3 Is businesslike	1 ② 3 4 ⑸ 6 7	Is slipshod
4 Interested in individuals	① ⑵ 3 4 5 6 7	Not interested in individuals

Step 5   There are several possible follow-ups to this exercise.
As an individual you can ask yourself:

- How do I compare with my ideal teacher?
- Will/Should I change on any of these dimensions?
- Which categories are most worthy of further scrutiny?

In a group you can consider:

- How do group members' views of ideal teachers differ from each other (the circled numbers)?
- What features are in common?
- How different from each other are individual members of the group on their self-ratings (the crossed numbers)?

One approach in a group is for the group leader to synthesise all members' views into a 'master list' of ten pairs of those opposites that appear in various guises in several people's individual lists. Then participants can each rate their own ideal teacher on such a master list and compare the results wit

h those of other members of the group, discussing

Step 6   ACTION   The final stage is to translate analysis into action. First of all, work out what each of your conclusions means in terms of *classroom behaviour*. Reflection on characteristics means little unless you decide what you must *do* to improve practice. Here are two examples of conclusions based on the examples on page 10 and how someone might translate these into action.

Conclusion: Need to be a bit more strict

Think about this first. Why do you need to be more strict? If children are misbehaving it may be because the work is boring, unsuitable, over- or under-demanding, rather than because you are too 'soft'.

Possible action includes:

- Deal with misbehaviour as soon as it occurs.
- Make fair use of punishments when appropriate, but also praise good behaviour.
- Clarify classroom rules about movement, talking, setting out of work, etc.
- Make sure the task is suitable, clearly defined and children know what they are supposed to be doing.
- Discuss with pupils what sort of misbehaviour is not right, and what steps children should take to be responsible for their own good behaviour.

Conclusion: Need to be more businesslike

If you decide this, then you need to ask yourself why, and also what you understand by 'business-like'. Do you forget to bring the right materials and books? Are your instructions to the class not clear? Don't you monitor and record children's work effectively?

Possible action includes:

- Prepare lessons more carefully.
- List requirements such as books and materials beforehand and make sure they are available.
- Work out in advance which the key points are that you wish to stress when you give instructions or explanations.
- Improve the organisation of the beginnings and endings of lessons.
- Look at the layout of the room and consider how appropriate it is for the activities taking place.

Class management is what teachers do to ensure that children engage in the task in hand

Unit 2 Different views

Given the different subject specialisms and traditions, temperaments, views, experiences and backgrounds of secondary teachers, it would be astonishing if all of them responded to the challenge of managing a class in the same way. Though there may, in certain cases, be broad similarities between teachers in the way they handle a disruptive event, or organise a project, there will also be significant differences.

Activity 2

Look at the picture on page 14. It shows a class of children entering the room in a boisterous manner. It is a picture we have used with hundreds of trainee, experienced and supply teachers. Each was asked to comment on the situation with the following storyline:

It is time for the second half of the morning on your first day with this class. They come running back into the room, pushing each other, squealing and laughing. What, if anything, do you do?

Consider and discuss the responses by the four teachers below:

Teacher A
This is only likely to happen at the beginning of the school year if I'm not present, which I usually am. I absolutely lay down the law about coming into the changing rooms and gyms [he was a teacher of physical education]. I make it quite clear that nobody has ever fooled about in my classes, so I don't propose to let it happen now. I never have much bother after that.

Teacher B
The most important discipline is self-discipline. I always try to be present when the class arrives, but you can't always be there. They've got to learn to come in and get on with their work even if I'm delayed, so I'd ask them a question, 'If you rush into a classroom like an unruly mob, what's going to happen before long?' They soon see for themselves that they've got to take some responsibility for avoiding accidents. You just have to bung the idea in.

teachers, who are firmly in charge and give numerous directions, whom one could not describe as lacking kindliness, understanding or concern for the child as an individual. In Victorian times, great stress was laid on the authority of the teacher and classes frequently chanted in unison learned answers to standard questions. Teachers were expected to exercise firm control over behaviour and the knowledge children acquired, and corporal punishment was used extensively. In more recent times, corporal punishment has been abandoned and the role of the teacher has come under close scrutiny, with vigorous debate about whether what is taught should be determined by the class teacher, fashioned by the children themselves or laid down centrally by statute.

Geoffrey Bantock (1965) asserts what for him is the inescapable 'authority' of the teacher in his book *Freedom and Authority in Education.*

> The teacher, however much he may attempt to disguise the fact, must, if only because he is not appointed or dismissed by pupils, represent an authority. He must do so, also because he is inescapably 'other' than the children. For one thing, he is older; he has inevitably undergone experiences which give him a different background of assumption from that of his charges. He is, that is to say, psychically different. He has, too, certain legal responsibilities and is answerable to the community at large for aspects of his behaviour. There is therefore unavoidably, mechanically, as it were, a gulf which no attempt at disguise can hide, because it is endemic in the situation, 'given'. Nor do I think that it should be disguised. Power is an inescapable element in adult life, to which we all at some time or other have to come to terms; and I deprecate a great deal of the current insincerity which strives to hide the true situation and thus prepares the child for a fictitious world, not one of reality, even when the circumstance is blanketed under some such grandiose title as 'training in the self-responsibilities of citizenship'. It is to be deprecated for a number of reasons, not least of which is the need to learn respect for the idea of authority as such, as a necessary element in the proper functioning of the community.

Typical classroom behaviour

Teachers would expect to make many of the decisions about content and procedure, with perhaps fewer explanations or justification of the reasons for such decisions. There may be less permitted movement or talking to other pupils. More directions would be given with the intention that they be carried out. Hand raising before speaking would be insisted upon, while disobedience would be punished with whatever agreed school sanctions are available.

Comments   Supporters of this mode of management argue that chaos ensues unless a teacher is clearly 'in charge', that children themselves expect teachers to be strict (see page 22), that teachers have the experience to know what children should be doing. Critics argue that authoritarian teaching can easily become repressive, that children need to learn to manage and determine their own behaviour if our rapidly changing society is to be truly democratic.

2 Democratic

The words 'democracy' and 'democratic' are often highly emotive and are usually regarded as indicating the polar opposite of 'authoritarian'. Children's freedom to develop autonomy, it is argued, will be inhibited by undue interference from the teacher. Again it is easy to stereotype, arguing that democracy is *ipso facto* the sort of approved behaviour that civilised people should endorse, or to use the word 'permissive' instead and assert that it is bound to lead to chaos. The following extract from A. S. Neill's *Summerhill* illustrates this concept in a form that has been influential in some schools, but rarely copied in its original form.

> Summerhill is a self-governing school, democratic in form. Everything connected with social, or group, life, including punishment for social offences, is settled by vote at the Saturday night General School Meeting.
>
> Each member of the teaching staff and each child, regardless of his age, has one vote. My vote carries the same weight as that of a 7-year-old.
>
> One may smile and say, 'But your voice has more value, hasn't it?' Well, let's see. Once I got up at a meeting and proposed that no child under 16 should be allowed to smoke. I argued my case: a drug, poisonous, not a real appetite in children, but mostly an attempt to be grown up. Counter-arguments were thrown across the floor. The vote was taken. I was beaten by a large majority.
>
> The sequel is worth recording. After my defeat, a boy of 16 proposed that no one under 12 should be allowed to smoke. He carried his motion. However, at the following weekly meeting a boy of 12 proposed the repeal of the new smoking rule, saying, 'We are all sitting in the toilets smoking on the sly just like kids do in a strict school, and I say it is against the whole idea of Summerhill.' His speech was cheered, and that meeting repealed the law. I hope I have made it clear that my voice is not always more powerful than that of a child.

Typical classroom behaviour

Teachers are less likely to issue commands, use reprimands or punishment. Freedom of movement is more permissible and the buzz of conversation among pupils may be louder. Emphasis will be more on pupils taking responsibility for their own behaviour.

Comments   Supporters argue that much of the management in Victorian times was repressive and produced too many uninventive and compliant adults, that children are perfectly capable of sensible behaviour, provided they are trusted. Critics claim that permissiveness too frequently degenerates into a laissez-faire ad-hoc sort of classroom where anything goes and little time is spent on learning, where social chit-chat can consume much of the time in school, at the expense of what the children are supposed to be studying.

Activity 3		
	1	Compare the quotes from Bantock and Neill on pages 16 and 17.
	2	Which parts of each do you agree and disagree with?
3		Are the two viewpoints completely irreconcilable polar opposites of each other?

3 Behaviour modification

The systematic modification of children's behaviour has often been controversial. This approach is based on the learning theories developed by B. F. Skinner and his associates. We learn best, it is believed, when positive behaviour is *reinforced*, often by reward or recognition. Thus, children who seek attention and are 'told off' are actually being encouraged to misbehave further to attract more attention. The role of the teacher is to help children to learn socially desirable behaviour.

Typical classroom behaviour

Teachers will ignore anti-social behaviour, on the grounds that failure to reinforce it by giving it attention will lead to its *extinction*, and they reward or publicly recognise approved behaviour, sometimes by giving out tokens, in the belief that this *reinforces* it and makes it more likely to occur. One of many adaptations of this approach is sometimes referred to as 'assertive discipline'. Rules are written up on the board and pupils who observe them (attend punctually, pay attention, desist from distracting others, for example) are given rewards, like pens, sweets, or certificates, while those who break the rules may have their privileges withdrawn or their name may be displayed in public.

Comments   This form of management has been criticised (Freiberg, 1999a), partly because it has sometimes been used in conjunction with certain drugs like ritalin, a stimulant given to children judged to be hyperactive or to lack attentiveness. Critics argue that the treatment is mechanistic, seeing people as machines, not humans; that formal reward systems of this kind are mere bribery, and that it is too overt a manipulation of young people. They also say that ignoring misbehaviour does not necessarily improve it and that, in the case of children who use swearwords, for example, 'reinforcement' may come from other pupils. Supporters counter this by saying that most teachers, and indeed most human beings in their relationships generally, use reinforcement techniques, and it is dishonest to pretend otherwise; that many children have learned to behave badly and want to behave well if only someone will show them how, and that 'contract' systems, whereby children specify what they themselves would like to achieve, have removed the 'teacher manipulation' objection. Andy Miller (1996) consulted educational psychologists about programmes they ran for children who were thought to be a problem in school. Nearly 90 per cent of them stated that their initial assessment involved assessing what was happening in terms of the pupil's behaviour.

4   Interpersonal relationships

The belief here is that learning takes place where positive relationships exist between a teacher and class and among pupils. The teacher's role is to develop a healthy classroom climate within which learning will automatically thrive. This approach is often much influenced by the views of Carl Rogers and his followers (Rogers and Freiberg, 1994, Freiberg, 1999a). A study of trainee teachers by Kyriacou (1997) reports that the students often aspired to this kind of humanistic view, but said, after teaching practice, that they had found it difficult to implement, especially with pupils who did not seem able to take responsibility for their own behaviour. This is not necessarily an argument against having such an ideal; it can equally be seen as an indication of the high degree of competence and commitment needed to carry it through.

Typical classroom behaviour

Teachers put a premium on personal relationships both between themselves and pupils and among pupils. There will, therefore, be more involvement of children in, say, the negotiation of rules, with discussion and suggestion about why these make sense. When problems occur, the teacher may employ what Glasser (1969) called 'reality therapy'. This enables children to have a personal interview with a teacher of their choice, someone with whom they have a strong rapport, to establish what is going wrong and why, what the consequences are of pupils' attitudes and actions, and how they might proceed in future.

Comments   Supporters of this point of view regard personal relationships as of crucial importance to all human society and argue, therefore, that children must learn how to establish positive relationships with their peers and with adults from an early age. They point out that difficult situations and events are frequently managed well in classrooms where relationships are good, but that similar events cause severe problems in classes where relationships are already poor. Critics counter that this can easily be overstated, that the pursuit of good relationships can begin to override the acquisition of skills and knowledge, and that there are classrooms where relationships are sound but where little is learned.

5   Scientific

Professor Nate Gage of Stanford University, in his books *The Scientific Basis of the Art of Teaching* and *Hard Gains in the Soft Sciences* (Gage, 1978 and 1985), put forward the proposition that teaching is a science as well as an art, and that teaching can be systematically studied and analysed. Once we know enough, he argued, behaviour can be predicted and 'successful' strategies identified. Jacob Kounin (1970), in his book *Discipline and Group Management in Classrooms*, used systematic observation of videotapes of primary classrooms to identify what he called 'desist' techniques – that is, action by teachers which seemed to be particularly effective when children misbehaved. He did not identify one single 'desist' as supremely effective, but rather described a series of strategies that were used by teachers who appeared to be successful at managing misbehaviour. He gave these strategies somewhat offbeat names like:

withitness   having eyes in the back of your head, thus picking up misbehaviour early.

overlapping   being able to do more than one thing at once: for example, deal with someone misbehaving while at the same time keeping the children you are with occupied.

smoothness   keeping children at work by *not*

    (a) intruding suddenly when they are busy (*thrusts*);

    (b) starting one activity and then leaving it abruptly to engage in another one (*dangles*);

    (c) ending an activity and then coming back to it unexpectedly (*flip-flops*).

overdwelling   skilful teachers avoided staying on an issue for longer than was necessary.

ripple effect   when a teacher interacted with an individual or a small group, 'Haven't you started yet, Mary?', 'That's a nice picture, John', the effect rippled outwards to others nearby who 'read' the messages: 'This teacher expects us to have started', 'This teacher is interested in our work'.

Typical classroom behaviour

This depends on what classroom research has been brought to teachers' attention, but, in the case of Kounin's successful 'desist' strategies described above, a teacher applying the principle of 'withitness', for example, during a PE lesson, might occasionally glance rapidly round the whole area to make sure all pupils are engaged in their task. While teaching art the teacher might decide to make a quick tour of the classroom immediately the children had begun work, commenting publicly on one or two individuals to exploit the 'ripple effect', giving a message to the whole class about what is expected, what is highly regarded or what is not permitted.

Comments   Critics argue that teaching is an art and cannot be analysed or taught in any systematic way, that there is, as yet, not sufficient research evidence to constitute a science of teaching, and that teachers are more influenced by their own personal experience than by what they read in research reports. Supporters point out that medieval doctors defended the use of leeches on similar grounds, that research evidence is necessary if teaching is to move forward, and that rather than replace a teacher's artistry, carefully collected evidence can form what Gage called a 'scientific basis' to enhance it.

6 Social systems

People in school are believed to belong to a subsystem of a wider social organisation in which many influences are at work on the group's behaviour. These may be political, social, financial, emotional, etc. Failure to understand these processes, it is said, will inhibit the teacher's ability to work effectively in a school, although learning itself is seen as an individual process.

Typical classroom behaviour

It is difficult to translate this belief into behavioural terms, but the teacher would probably be interested in the wider aspects of education, be knowledgeable about the school's catchment area, the family background, religious beliefs and community traditions and values. Gillborn and Youdell (2000), for example, studied teachers' uses of target setting with pupils taking General Certificate of Secondary Education examinations at the age of 16. They found that teachers concentrated on students who had obtained grade D in the 'mock' examinations, as they were seen as the ones most likely to reach the more highly desired grade A, B and C category. The students deemed to be below grade D, often from working class and ethnic minority backgrounds, were likely to be ignored, in some cases even omitted from pupil lists. In primary classrooms it would be equally easy to succumb to external pressures, such as performance tables, and concentrate on pupils who were borderline, while neglecting the rest. There are other phases of secondary schooling when it is also likely that teachers may concentrate on borderline pupils.

Comments   Many school problems, argue those interested in this aspect, cannot be dealt with in isolation. Poor housing, financial hardship, family circumstances, parents' employment or lack of it, their education, aspirations and attitudes, all these may exert more powerful influences over pupils' behaviour than anything that happens in school. Teachers need to know about the religious beliefs of the children in their classes, for example, so that they understand why a child might be away from school celebrating a particular festival, or why there might be a particular view of diet, physical education and dance, or family life. Critics counter by saying that teachers have little or no control over these external factors, and, while able to be sympathetic and understanding, must of necessity act within the framework of the school. Hence the complaint sometimes heard from teachers at conferences, 'I am a teacher, not a social worker'.

7 Folklore

Teachers over the years have built up a stock of 'tricks of the trade'. These can be learned, it is said, and the young teacher will be equipped with an omni-purpose set of recipes, which will be useful in most situations. The most common tips reported by teachers and students interviewed during our research projects included: 'Prepare and plan carefully', 'Be well organised and anticipate problems', 'Develop different strategies for different ages of children', 'Establish good personal relationships', 'Be firm in your guidelines, and let children know the limits', 'Keep children busy'.

Typical classroom behaviour

Once more this depends on the kind of folklore which has been purveyed, but beginning teachers offered the common tip 'start strictly and ease off later' may well attempt to be more severe than they might otherwise have been in the early stages.

Comments   Those who believe in tips claim that considerable accumulated professional wisdom lies behind them, that such tips are fairly universal in many schools and cultures, and that generations of trainees have gratefully acknowledged their value. Critics say that tips are lacking in any theoretical basis, are random and unrelated to each other, and may suit the person who proffers them, but not the recipient.

PUPILS' VIEWS

Pupils at school have a clear and consistent view of their ideal teacher or of teachers they regard as incompetent (Wragg *et al.*, 2000). Surveys over a long period of time, since the 1930s, show that, in general, pupils expect teachers to be slightly strict, rather than very strict or permissive. They expect fair use of rewards and punishments, and anyone who needs confirmation of this should simply ask elderly friends and relatives in their seventies or eighties to recall their schooldays. They frequently remember in vivid detail events of their childhood in school, especially where unfairness is involved, for this in particular leaves an abiding impression. Children also prefer teachers whose lessons are interesting, who see them as individuals, who can explain things clearly and who have a sense of humour, but do not engage in sarcasm.

In summary, children tend to prefer teachers who:

- are slightly strict, but not over-severe or permissive
- are fair in their use of rewards and punishments
- treat them as individuals
- are interesting and provide a variety of stimulating work
- are friendly and good humoured, but not sarcastic
- explain things clearly

Pupil fiddling with geometry instruments

Activity 4

Look at the picture above showing a pupil fiddling noisily with his geometry instruments. The teacher finds that he often does this at the beginning of a lesson. Make a list below of how teachers with different beliefs, influences and practices, as described on page 15 onwards, might respond, and then consider what you think would be the consequences of the action or inaction. If you are working with a group of teachers, compare your responses with those of other participants. Decide what this tells you about your own preferences and your likely response to actual classroom behaviour. A sample (but not a model!) response has been entered in the pro-forma overleaf.

Finally, consider any particular ideas you might try out in your own teaching in future. An example – one of numerous possibilities – is given below, but you should test out your ideas in the light of your own analysis. Remember the labels 'authoritarian', 'democratic', 'scientific', etc., have sometimes acquired emotive overtones. They are used here for general convenience, and are not meant to be hard-edged stereotypes. Indeed, the notion 'authoritarian' must be dry cleaned of its association with peremptory and insensitive behaviour and it must be recognised that 'scientific' does not imply the precision normally accorded to the hard sciences.

Example ('Scientific' category)

It has often been found that teachers who took action to deal with misbehaviour early were less likely to have problems than those who allowed it to escalate. If you do not normally take action early, try nipping misbehaviour problems in the bud and then reflect on the outcome.

TEACHER RESPONSE

The teacher decides this is 'attention-seeking' and so ignores it, so as not to reinforce it. However, she waits until the boy commences work and then congratulates him for making a positive start (behaviour modification).

Write more responses below.

POSSIBLE OUTCOMES

It might work as planned, reinforcing positive behaviour reducing the attention seeking, but it might not be 'attention seeking' in the first place, so the teacher would need to find out why he fiddles with his pencil case (does he not understand what he is supposed to do?)

Write more possible outcomes below.

Activity 5

Step 1   Show the picture on page 14 to pupils in one of your classes. Ask them the following questions, and then discuss their answers with them. If you are a student or supply teacher, make sure that the head and class teacher do not mind your doing this exercise with pupils.

'I want you to think of the best teacher in the whole world. Try to imagine someone who is a brilliant teacher. Now look at this picture. These children rush into the classroom pushing each other out of the way, knocking things over and making a lot of noise. What do you think this brilliant teacher would do if that happened?

Step 2   Use another picture or make up another storyline and ask children what the imaginary 'perfect teacher' would do.

Step 3   Think about the children's responses to these situations. Do they surprise you? Or are they what you expected? Do they make you think about your own handling of similar situations?

Step 4   (only for the courageous) Ask some children about their views on the 'perfect teacher' and then ask them how they think you are (a) similar and (b) different. (Have a stiff drink ready for afterwards, in case you need it.)

Many schools invest time and energy at the beginning of the school year to establish a climate which, they hope, will last through the year. There may be mention in the first assembly of the need for high achievement – good behaviour, tidiness, thought for others, or whatever the school wishes to stress. Individual teachers will then immediately reinforce, or occasionally confound, these aspirations in their own classrooms. In interview before the start of the school year, experienced heads and teachers are usually very clear about what they will do at the beginning of the school year. There are two groups of teachers, however, who do not have the same advantages as full-time class teachers. These are supply teachers and students on school experience or teaching practice. Supply teachers often have considerable teaching experience and clarity in their own minds about such matters as classroom rules, but have to manage numerous first encounters at various stages of the school year, without the benefit of the collective effort made by others in early September. Student teachers suffer a double disadvantage. They, too, arrive partway through the school year, and therefore miss the support of the whole school's initial effort of the previous September, but in addition they are often unsure about what their own rules should be and what sort of relationships they will seek to establish.

First meetings with classes go through a predictable series of stages, albeit with considerable individual variations according to the school's and teacher's preferred style, the age, nature and size or the class, and certain unpredictable events. The sequence is made up of six key phases of varying length, intensity and importance: preparation and forethought; entry into school; entry into classroom or home base; teacher's opening words; first few minutes of lesson; early phase.

1 Preparation and forethought

In some cases teachers are able to meet their 'new' class at the end of the previous school year, either as a group or individually. This is not always possible, however, and in any case the first sustained encounter is likely to occur when the teacher or student takes over the class on a more permanent basis. Consider these three teachers talking about their preparation for their first day with a class:

Teacher A (Drama teacher)

The first impression I give is of tight, purposeful, nervous energy. The children learn to expect this. I try to create a feeling that something's going to happen, even if I don't know what I'm going to do …It's important to be hard in the first lesson. By 'hard' I mean a body thing, creating a shroud of mystery. I don't allow the kids to pierce it thoroughly until later.

Teacher B (Student teacher)

Ideally I'd like a fairly intimate relationship with the class, but I realise that that requires drawing a line between intimacy and cheek, a fine balance I'd like to achieve. I don't know how. I haven't given it a lot of thought. It's important. I need to think about it.

Teacher C (Supply teacher)

Basically if I'm approaching a new class, I'm getting myself ready to get in there fairly early – I'm usually in a half hour, forty minutes, before I actually meet a class, because you want to put over the idea that you're well organised and a together person. I think the worst thing a supply can do is to be dithery in front of a new class. It's important that you are competent and confident with taking a register …You've got to get a bit of street credibility fairly early on, I think.

Activity 6

1   Compare the statements by Teachers A, B and C.
2   What control is each likely to have over such matters as room layout, emotional tone, curriculum-related activities, discipline?
3   What are the general differences between experienced teachers starting with a new class in September and supply teachers or student teachers meeting a new class in mid-year?
4   The experienced teachers above talk about impression management. How important is 'image'? Should teachers behave differently when they first meet their new classes?

2 Entry into school

This is where whole school policy can be important. Many secondary schools make sure they are highly organised on the very first day of the new school year, though some appear more chaotic. In one school we observed there was considerable disorganisation on entry and individual teachers appeared to be struggling to establish order in the first few minutes of their first session with their new classes. In many schools, children are escorted in by the head and staff and there is a well-defined procedure for commencing the school year, either with a set of reception routines or with an assembly.

The first school assembly in schools is often one in which there is some kind of exhortation. It may be direct or indirect, by instruction or through a story. In one of our research projects observers studied the first week of the school year in twenty schools. Among the themes, statements and events that were recorded, in addition to the hymns and prayers, were the following, which illustrate a range of purposes: control, inspiration, informing, laying down of rules, outlining of expectations, establishment or reinforcement of school ethos, assertion of community values:

- The head announced improvements in national test scores and encouraged all pupils to strive for even higher achievement: 'We're expecting great things of you.'
- The deputy head harangued one of the older year groups about their behaviour during the previous year and appealed to them to give a lead to younger pupils.
- A theme 'what is respect?' was introduced.
- The head looked round at some of the new pupils, asking them their names and which primary school they had attended, commenting when they were younger siblings of older pupils, or saying, 'We've had some very good pupils from there.'
- Some older pupils stood up and talked about taking care of others who need help.
- Discouragement from coming to school very early, as 'you will not be allowed into the building.'
- The head got angry with a small group of pupils who were not listening and then paused dramatically until they paid attention.

3 Entry into classroom

During the first hour or two of the new school year there is usually a high level of excitement, even among the disaffected. Pupils returning to school after a gap of several weeks are eager to find out who is in their class, what their friends did on holiday and who is sitting where. There is often a rush for seats, or else children stand talking by the door, uncertain what is happening. Some teachers insist on an orderly line-up outside the classroom, talk to pupils in the corridor or whatever space the queue occupies, accompany them into the room, assign places and move on to the next phase, while others are more distant. A fuss may be made about orderly behaviour; one teacher we observed shouting, 'You don't call that lined up, do you? LINE UP!'

Step 1   Read the following report of the first morning at school in a class of 11-year-olds, starting secondary school for the first time.

The school is a large comprehensive on the edge of a city. From eight o'clock large numbers of pupils begin to appear, some alone, others in twos and threes. Most 11-year-olds have come from small- to medium-sized primary schools, with about a fifth of the numbers of their new school. Buses arrive and disgorge large numbers of young passengers, some disembarking slowly and blearily, others more boisterously. Cars pull up at intervals and individuals or pairs of children emerge. The road in front of the school becomes congested and cars double park, blocking the road. The headteacher stands at the gate, greeting familiar faces, quizzing newcomers amiably. Soon most of the children are in school and the street outside is quieter apart from occasional late arrivals.

Mr B is a very experienced science teacher and a head of department. At eleven o'clock he has his first class of new pupils. They enter the laboratory in an orderly manner. He does not comment on their entry, but starts with a question, 'Can anyone see anything dangerous in here?' Most pupils are too apprehensive to reply, but some venture responses:

'There's a lot of glass.'

'Yes, good, anything else?'

'Gas taps.'

'Right. What else?'

'Bottles with poison in them.'

'Yes, well, it's mostly poisonous and some of it could give you a nasty burn. Can you think what might burn you?'

'Acid.'

'That's right, acid, like this [picks up bottle and holds it up]. Looks like water, doesn't it, but never be fooled by appearances. You'll learn to look very carefully at things in my science lessons. Now, I want you all to go out again and come in as quietly and orderly as you can. We don't want any accidents, so you'll always come in properly. Off you go … steady.'

Step 2 Imagine you are an 11-year-old and it is your very first day in your new school. How do you think you might react to the following?

- Headteacher greeting people at the gate.
- Only a few familiar faces; most are strangers.
- Large numbers of pupils, almost all of whom are older and bigger.
- First entry into a science laboratory.
- First lesson with your new science teacher.

Step 3 Consider and discuss the next few minutes of Mr B's science lesson, as described by the observer who watched it. What do you think of his way of stressing safe conduct? Would you tackle the issue differently?

Pupils re-enter the lab in an orderly manner. Mr B comments, 'That's better' (even though they had entered in an orderly manner the first time!). 'Now I want you to make sure you always come in like that.' He gives out a sheet of paper. 'I said this was a dangerous place, so here's what I want you to do.' He then distributes a sheet of paper listing the 'official' safety requirements laid down by the local authority and says, 'Right. Now these are the safety rules for our science lessons, so I want you to read each of them through and decide why you think we do that. Why is it a rule?' As the class writes down their ideas, he patrols around the lab, commenting occasionally on what they have written.

4   Teacher's opening words

Most teachers use voice and posture to secure attention in their very first lesson. They usually establish some kind of central presence and then make a 'public voice' statement. Often this is an exhortation to stop talking, a check on attendance, or an invitation to start on the content of the lesson. A wide range of opening statements has been recorded during our own research studies, including the following:

> 'Right, sit down quickly, we've a lot to get through today, so put your bags away and pay attention to me. Quickly now.'

> 'I've got a very funny name, so we're all going to have a good laugh ...Everyone get ready to laugh ...You don't look ready to laugh.'

> 'I'm letting you sit where you want for the time being, so don't fuss, settle down.'

> 'Is everybody here now? Who's missing? Anybody got lost on the way?'

> 'You've all got your books, haven't you? Anyone not got a book? Good ... today we'll be doing matrices.'

These varied statements show a little of the range of purposes and strategies for obtaining attention, depending on the context. If children settled quickly, a friendly opening, setting a relaxed social climate, was frequently used. If they milled around in confusion, a much more staccato response resulted, often incorporating an order or command, like the teacher who shouted, as children bunched by the door, chattering noisily, 'Don't worry about pegs and bags, go into the classroom quietly and stand behind a chair, any chair.' Attention was usually sought to take a register, but seating, allocation of seats or social chat also featured.

Pupil responses were also varied. In most cases there was a positive response and the children fell quiet or obeyed instructions. In a few cases where they did not, teachers usually reacted immediately, sometimes by simply calling out the name of the misbehaving pupil(s), sometimes by standing with hands on hips until there was silence, occasionally with mild sarcasm ('I hope you at the back heard what I said').

5   The first lesson

One significant difference is often detected between students and experienced teachers in the context of first encounters. Students tend to concentrate most on the subject content or topic of first lesson activities, whereas experienced teachers spend more time and effort establishing a climate, assigning seating, usually on a free or 'moderated' choice basis, with the teacher exercising the occasional right of veto, giving out books, explaining facilities and equipment in the room, and the eventual activity seems to be of secondary importance at this initial stage.

Students are well aware that they are entering someone else's established set of routines, so they often seek to make their own individual impression, talking about 'a game', 'something dramatic like a fountain', 'a magic poetry machine that would make them look forward to the next time'. Others opt for something safe, like this geography student teaching about Australia:

> 'I'll introduce it and talk about it for a while, quite a conventional type of lesson, not flashy because it might go wrong and the kids will remember, quite a safe lesson, a good conventional approach. I'd leave the flashy things till later on when I knew them better.'

6 The early phase

The first few lessons with a class have to serve a wide variety of purposes. There are inescapable classroom rituals, like seating, registration, books and materials to be dealt with; in addition, teachers are conscious of the need to lay down rules of conduct (see Unit 4), establish a working and social climate, signal what level of noise they will tolerate, deal with personal problems, pupils new to the school, uncertainties or queries from parents.

Whereas teachers of older pupils can often take for granted that children will know the school's routines and expectations, though they may need reminding of them, new classes, often fresh from comparatively small primary schools, have to be inducted into the school and specialist subject teaching for the very first time, with all the sociological complexities that implies. Someone who six weeks previously was being taught by a single teacher and was a senior, is now a junior with perhaps ten different specialists, working in what is often a more formal and structured environment. 'You, what's your name?' the teacher asks when some new 11-year-old wanders across the room. 'Er, Stephen.' 'Stephen what?' 'Stephen Carter.' 'Well, sit down, Stephen. You don't leave your seat without permission in my class.' It is often firm but kindly. It is certainly different.

Student and supply teachers are spared that side of induction, but have to read numerous messages, risk confusing children by introducing routines at variance with what they are used to, or indeed, may themselves become confused by children's accounts, real or mischievous, of what is normally expected.

Activity 8

Imagine you are taking a class for the first time, or, if you are about to take a real new class, address the questions below with that class in mind.

1   What would you like to know about the class in advance, and why?
2   What sort of topic or theme will you choose for this first lesson and why?
3   What will you be doing and thinking about:

   (a)   an hour before the lesson?
   (b)   five minutes before the lesson?

4   Do you plan to be present before the class arrives, if this is possible? If not, why not?

5   If you are present outside the room or home base before the session begins, what will you be doing:

    (a)   before entering the room?
    (b)   as the children enter the room?

6   How will you begin the lesson:

    (a)   if the class settles down quickly?
    (b)   if the class is slow to settle?

7   How do you think the class will see you on first meeting you?

8   Are there any rules you will want to establish from the beginning? (and why are these your most pressing rules?)

9   What kind of relationship would you like to have with the class in the longer term, and how will you set about establishing it?

10   What teaching strategies, so far as you can see, will you employ during the first session – groupwork? individual assignments? whole class teaching? question and answer? writing? reading? giving instructions?

Activity 9

If you are taking a new class, analyse your first session with them in the light of your plans in Activity 8.

A   Preparation and planning

How effective was your preparation? Was there information you would have liked about the children but did not get?

B   Lesson beginning

Were you present when the class arrived? What happened? How did they enter the room? How did you introduce yourself? Did the class settle down quickly?

C   First impression

What do you think was the class's first impression of you? Circle a point on the scales below:

Brisk, businesslike	1 2 3 4 5 6 7	Slipshod
Warm, friendly	1 2 3 4 5 6 7	Aloof
Stimulating	1 2 3 4 5 6 7	Dull

Is this what you would like in the longer term? If not, what can you do to change children's perceptions of you? What do you think children told their parents about their new teacher when they got home?

D   Rules
What school and classroom rules emerged, either because you stated them or because you reacted to some event?

E   Content
You may not have been able to spend much time on your actual topic or lesson content in your first session, but how did children react to their first task? Were they busy? Bored? Confused? Intrigued? Indifferent? How did the session end?

F   Names
Think of the class concerned and write in the space below the names of any pupils to whom you can put a face.

G   Follow-up action
Ask yourself the following:

1   Are your rules the same as other teachers'? How do children know what is and what is not permitted?

2   To what extent does your first session reflect the kind of relationship you would like with the class in the longer term? What should you do in future lessons to establish the sort of relationships you wish to have?

3   Look at your answers to F above. Which children's names do you know and why do you know these? Did they misbehave? Have you taught them before? See if you can learn all the children's names soon. Consider those children whose names come less easily to mind and see if you can get to know them better. Who are they? Are they new? Or just quiet and well behaved?

First lesson and first day endings

Just as first encounters have an opening, so they have a conclusion, and lesson and day endings can be just as important as beginnings, for closure is something that will happen every day of the year. In most of the first encounters we have observed, the ending of the first session and the first day were slightly more formal than subsequent days. Classes were usually dismissed as a whole during the day, sometimes according to how still they were sitting at the end of the day, and asked to walk in an orderly fashion. In laboratory, workshop and practical lessons equipment had to be cleared away, though not all teachers anticipated this, nor did they all alert their class to the passage of time.

Many lessons had a formal act of closure, but not in every case. Sometimes there was a systematic review of what had been done, what had supposedly been learned, or a report back from groups or individuals, but again this was not always in evidence, though some teachers made a question and answer review a regular ending to their subsequent lessons. Occasionally there was some closing comment and anticipation of future work: 'That's good. You've done very well today. Now tomorrow we'll be ...'.

Pupils' personal needs

There are several issues that are quite important for pupils but may be overlooked by teachers. For new classes especially there may be some anxiety about the conventions in their new school and how quickly they can learn these. It may concern something simple like cleanliness or toilet conventions. What do you do, pupils will want to know, if you want to wash your hands or go to the toilet? Can you just go? Must you ask the teacher? A host of other minor matters may also be in children's minds: Where do you hang your coat? Is it in order to have your bag on the table? the floor? What happens at registration? Assembly? Dinner time? Break time? How should work be set out? These issues will also be addressed in Unit 4.

Activity 10

1   Make a list of matters to do with classroom routines and personal needs which you may need to consider.

2   How will you communicate to children what they should do or what you expect or permit?

3   Are any of these matters a special problem? If so, what can you do about it?

Unit 4   The two Rs – rules and relationships

Many human activities are governed by rules, some explicit and often available in written form, others implicit, unwritten, unspoken even. If we were to try to play a game like chess without observing the rules it would either consist of constant negotiation, or it would be chaotic, or it would collapse under a welter of argument. On the other hand, few families have a written set of rules about mealtimes, television watching or use of the bathroom. Such codes as govern these family matters have often been worked out by trial and error, by sustained informal negotiation over a long period of time.

RULES

Life without any rules at all would be chaotic and downright dangerous. Too many pedantic and rigid rules, however, would paralyse a community, which is why workers in dispute with their employer sometimes decide to 'work to rule'. In an unruly society we would probably be killed crossing the road, for how could we know on which side of the road to expect cars and lorries, or indeed whether they might suddenly veer on to the footpath?

Rules in school are of several kinds. There are national rules, many incorporated in Acts of Parliament, which govern such matters as pupil attendance, parental rights, use of punishments; there are local authority rules, such as the code of laboratory safety, or what teachers must do on field trips; there are also school rules which may be similar to or different from those of other schools, and these can concern dress, behaviour in the playground or use of facilities. Finally, there are teachers' rules on matters such as talking, movement, the setting-out of work or disruptive behaviour.

The question of rules is closely bound up with, but also distinct from, that of relationships. The relationship between two or more people is to some extent affected by the rule conventions under which it operates. As Bantock (1965) said in the quotation on page 16, teachers are paid to be present and are therefore different from pupils. They also have legal and contractual obligations, to act as a parent, *in loco parentis*, which means that, to some extent, their relationship with children is affected by what a court might require of them. Should there be an accident, teachers can avoid legal action for negligence by acting as a responsible parent would, summoning help, checking that the child is in good hands, communicating with those who need to know. When sour relationships develop, it is sometimes because rules are perceived to be unfairly or inconsistently applied, or because there is dissent or uncertainty about the rules themselves.

Within the first few days of the school year, dozens of rules are established or reaffirmed in some form or another by teachers. However, although some rules are stated explicitly early in the school year, like the science lab safety issues mentioned above, it is common for others to emerge by case law: 'don't talk to your neighbour when someone is answering a question, listen', 'walk on the left please', 'you're not allowed to play football there', 'show your working clearly and underline each answer with a ruler'. Given the many rules and conventions governing behaviour in schools, it is hardly surprising that teachers do not attempt to read them all out on the first morning – it would be too much to recall and would suggest that school is solely about rules. Some rules may even be expressed through euphemism. When one teacher expressed dismay about someone who 'had big eyes', this was not a slur on Mickey Mouse, but rather a coded message that a pupil had been spotted looking at a neighbour's paper during a test.

One of the most frequent findings in our own research is the importance of *consistency*. Teachers who are consistent seem to have fewer difficulties than those who are inconsistent or erratic, tolerating misdemeanours on certain occasions, or from some pupils, but becoming cross about identical matters at other times. Professor Jerry Freiberg (Rogers and Freiberg, 1994) has worked with some of the most difficult schools in the United States to improve discipline. Consistent implementation of humane rules and the involvement of pupils in managing their own behaviour has been a very important part of his programmes, which have produced not only fewer referrals to the principal or exclusions for poor behaviour, but also a significant increase in performance in English and mathematics scores.

Let us now take, as an example, the common rule, 'Don't call out, put your hand up if you want to speak.' I have observed several different ways of establishing this, including the following:

Teacher A   'One thing I want everybody to be clear about in my class is that you must put your hand up whenever you want to say something. I don't want anyone calling out. If everyone calls out then we can't hear what anybody is saying.' (Early in the first lesson of the year.)

Teacher B   'What do we always do before we want to speak?'
(An odd one this. It happened early on the first day of school, and although teachers sometimes use 'we' when they mean 'you', it seemed especially strange in this context since she never raised her own hand. Moreover, when a pupil called out, 'Put your hand up', she replied, 'That's quite right, Alison,' even though Alison had, herself, called out – a mixed set of messages.)

Teacher C   'I'm getting a bit concerned about everybody just calling out, "Miss, Miss," all the time. Let's see you put your hands up and then I'll decide who speaks.' (On the second day, when the class had become noisy.)

Activity 11	

1   Write down the three or four most important rules you can think of for your own classroom.

(i)

(ii)

(iii)

(iv)

2   Write down some other, less important rules that occur to you.

(i)

(ii)

(iii)

(iv)

3   Discuss the following:

(i)   How would you classify each of your rules? (Movement? Property? Relationships? School work?)

(ii)   Why is your first set of rules more important than your second set?

(iii)   Take one or two of your more important rules and describe how you established them. (In written form? Did you tell people what you expected? Did you wait until the rule was broken and then react?)

(iv)   What do you do when someone breaks each of your rules?

(v)   How do your rules reflect on and affect your relationships with pupils?

There are certain differences as well as similarities here. All three teachers were seeking to achieve the same goal, that of persuading children to raise their hands before speaking, but whereas Teacher A stated this explicitly as a rule clearly on the first day, Teacher C waited until some degree of disorder occurred. Teacher A also gave an explanation, self-evident maybe, of why the rule existed.

Interviews with teachers and observations of lessons shows that rules fall under certain clear headings. These included the following, with some specific examples in each case.

Movement

Walk quietly.
No running.
Ask first if you want to go to the toilet.
Don't just wander around the room, unless you're getting something.

Talking

Don't talk when I'm talking to you.
You should only be talking to each other if it's about your work.
Don't talk when someone is answering a question.
Only one person talking at a time.
No shouting out.
Put your hands up, if you want to ask a question.
Silence during registration.
Silence in the library area.

Work-related

Being able to work independently on your own.
Being able to work harmoniously in a group.
Working quietly even if the teacher is out of the room.
Starting work without having to be told.
Not distracting or spoiling the concentration of others when they are working.
No mobile phones, or if permitted they must be switched off during lessons.

Presentation

Knowing how to set out work and when to hand it in.
Taking care with content.

Safety

Care with equipment, particularly in subjects like science, technology, PE.
No swinging on chairs, pushing and shoving.
No playing on slippery banks in wet weather.

Space

Not allowed in classrooms or specialist rooms at break.
Carrying out activities near appropriate facility (e.g. sink, bench, gym equipment).

Materials

Equipment to be handled carefully and kept in proper place.
Keep library books tidy.
Know the correct place for returning equipment or unused materials.
Put things away properly at the end of the day.
Clothing and PE equipment to be kept in the approved place.
No writing on desks or book covers.
Return borrowed items to their owner.
Stack chairs on or under tables or desks at the end of the day.

Social behaviour

Show consideration for others.
Be willing to share things and co-operate.
Don't abuse or take the property of classmates without permission.
Be polite and thoughtful, treat others as you would like to be treated yourself.
Show good manners.

Clothing/appearance

Clothing to be neat and clean.
Wear appropriate uniform properly (e.g. shirt tucked in).
All clothing to be labelled.
During hot weather sleeves may be rolled up, cardigans, jackets, pullovers and ties removed.
Hairstyles, jewellery, studs and rings only as approved.

Activity 12

1   Consider the sets of rules above. Which do you find most important and which seem more trivial? Which would you wish to see in operation in your own classroom, and which not?

2   Take some particular rules, perhaps 'safety requirements', 'consideration for others', 'being able to work independently on your own', or 'appropriate dress must be worn' and discuss how a teacher might (a) establish (b) explain the need for and (c) fine tune such a rule.

3   Choose some rules about which different teachers in the same school might disagree:

(a)   what problems might be caused by different practices

(b)   what solutions might be found to avoid difficulties. Such rules as 'not being allowed in classroom at break time', 'working quietly even if the teacher is out of the room' and 'knowing how to set out work and when to hand it in' are worth considering here.

4   Discuss the extent to which there should be uniformity and what degree of diversity is permissible in different teachers' classroom rules and conventions within the same school.

SELF-DISCIPLINE AND NEGOTIATION

Rules are usually imposed on children by adults. The idea of negotiating rules with them is not as widespread as one might believe. Yet in much of school, and indeed most of adult life, we have to take responsibility for discipline ourselves, in the light of society's established order, without some superordinate telling us what to do every few minutes. Most people agree that self-discipline is important and that pupils in school should master it, but this belief is not always translated into practices which would secure it. There are many ways in which pupils themselves can take more responsibility for their own and their colleagues' behaviour and progress, without the teacher abdicating responsibility.

There is a view proposed by Glasser (1969), in his book *Schools without Failure*, that class management problems are made easier if children can understand why certain rules apply, or are consulted about the sort of behaviour that is desirable in a classroom. Glasser argued that it was worthwhile for teachers to spend some time explaining what rules they believed in, but also asking pupils to suggest adjustments or new rules of their own. Subsequently, other proponents have suggested that teachers should discuss rule-related problems to see who 'owns' it, whether it was the teacher, the pupil, or a shared responsibility. This raises the issue about what *is* open to negotiation – bullying, theft, damage to property and people, for example? The means of prevention, perhaps, but surely not the issues themselves. Ensuring children's wellbeing and law-abiding behaviour is a legal requirement on teachers, for they must exercise the 'duty of care', as it is called.

Occasionally it may be worth creating the time for discussion of what is happening in the classroom, especially at the beginning of the year, or if there appear to be problems. This ritual is known as 'Circle Time' in primary schools, when pupils sit round and discuss the process of teaching and learning with their teacher. From time to time it may be a valuable lubricant in a secondary class, though not if it becomes an over-indulgence or begins to predominate.

There was an interesting variant to Mr B's way of giving out the local authority's rules on laboratory safety, described on page 31. Another teacher in the same school also began by saying that a laboratory could be a dangerous place, but he engaged the children's interest by giving them a blank piece of paper first, saying, 'I want you to make up and write down some rules which will help us avoid having accidents.' Most of the LEA rules like 'no running or pushing', 'handle equipment carefully', 'be careful with flames or acids', were anticipated by the class, so that when he gave out copies of the actual rules they were pleased at their success. Matters like 'wearing goggles', which no one had suggested, were then discussed.

One important fundamental question about negotiation is not merely what is or what should be negotiable, but how children can understand the need for rules, such as wearing proper clothing on a field trip, staying away from dangerous places and not taking risks. This does not negotiate away teachers' legal responsibilities, it actually makes them more meaningful. Adolescents need to face up to matters such as self-discipline and respect for others, because these are necessary in families and communities, as well as in schools. Teachers in the end must take responsibility for rules, even if they sometimes endorse sensible proposals from pupils.

There are several ways in which rules can be introduced. These include, with examples:

General explanation   'I want to see you showing consideration for others.'

Specific prescription   'You must put your hand up when you want to say something.'

Rule with explanation   'I don't want anyone pushing and shoving near that sink, because someone's going to spill water on the floor and slippery floors cause accidents.'

General question   'How can we make sure everyone gets a fair chance to do well in their exams next summer?'

Specific question   'What would happen if nobody in the school had name tags on their clothes?'

Case law   'Haven't you started yet?' 'I don't understand what we're supposed to do.' 'Well, if you're not clear about something you should put your hand up, instead of just sitting there waiting, and I'll come over and explain it to you.'

Negotiation   'I've allowed you to talk to each other while you're doing your projects, but it's getting far too noisy, so let's just discuss for a minute what we can do about it.'

Self-monitoring   'You'll have to make a lot of decisions yourself when you're older, so let's see how well you can manage your own work, without me having to tell you what to do all the time.'

Activity 13 Achievement and behaviour

This activity is designed to involve pupils in looking at certain aspects of their own behaviour in a mature way. From primary school right up to the end of secondary education many boys do less well than girls at school, especially in language-type activities and in terms of behaviour. Four or five times as many boys as girls are excluded from school for poor behaviour. Boys are also more likely to jeer at their fellows who appear to work hard in class, using terms like 'boff', 'boffin' or 'keano'. This activity is suitable for the younger pupils in a secondary school, older pupils need a modified approach. It should be completed at the beginning of the year, but it may be done later. Students or inexperienced teachers should only do this in close collaboration with someone more experienced. The form and wording will need to be modified according to the age, ability and background of the pupils.

1   Explain to the class that, as you will be working together in future, you all need to be clear about behaviour.
2   Ask orally, or in writing, for 'Reasons why we come to school', and then discuss these. Most children will give replies like, 'To learn to read and write' or, 'To help us get a job', but other answers like, 'Because we have to' are worth discussing.

3   Ask pupils to suggest or write down some simple rules of behaviour and procedure which will help everyone learn better. This will often produce suggestions like, 'Don't interfere with others who are working', or, 'Don't mess about.' Related matters can then be raised, like, 'What about when we're discussing something?' (no calling out, listen to others) or, 'What about when we're working in groups?' (share things, wait your turn, don't ridicule the efforts of others).

4   Ask if there are any differences between the ways that boys and girls behave in class. Discuss, in as sensitive a manner as possible, the common finding that in many schools girls are doing better academically than boys.

5   Get everyone to make a special effort to establish a climate that helps people learn and work harmoniously together.

RELATIONSHIPS

Rules and relationships can be closely connected. Much of what has been covered in this unit so far is not just a matter of rules but also of personal relationships. The following observation notes from contrasting events in lessons make this clear. Both concern pupils who were not working when they should have been, but the first is more benign in its exposition and enforcement than the second and creates a positive relationship, while the second achieves the opposite effect.

A   A girl has not started her work in a maths lesson. 'Don't you understand what I want?' the teacher asks. 'Oh yes. I understand what you want, but I don't see why,' she replies. The teacher stands by her and explains fully and carefully that it is an exercise in relationships and shapes, one with another. He has noticed that some people were making mistakes, did not know what to emphasise, or were not looking carefully. The girl listens attentively and, apparently quite satisfied, goes on with her work, looking very carefully.

B   The teacher is talking to the whole class in her science lesson when two boys begin to talk to each other. The teacher swings round rapidly, points and glares at one of the offending lads and barks out in a very loud and frightening voice, 'Did I ask you to talk?' He pauses for two seconds in the ensuing silence and stares. 'Well, don't then.' The boys stop talking and the observer notes that the rest of the class appears shocked. There had been a considerable change in the teacher's voice, strength and tempo.

Personal relationships between teacher and pupils can be shaped in many locations and contexts. Consider just some examples of these, both positive and negative in their effect.

Academic	Explaining patiently to pupil who does not understand a new concept.
	Making a sarcastic remark to someone who doesn't understand a new concept.
Managerial	Smiling at and thanking someone who has helped clear away.
	Blaming someone for mess, choosing the wrong pupil.

Personal relationships are important

Social	Chatting to pupils as they enter classroom about what they did at the weekend. Belittling someone's hobby or family/cultural interest.
Expectation	Looking for positive qualities and achievements in children. Having low expectations or always focusing on the negative side of pupils' work or behaviour.
Home/school/ community	Talking positively with parents and members of children's communities. Showing no interest in children's origins and values.
Individual	Taking a personal interest in children as individuals. Seeing class entirely as a group without individual identities.

Personal relationships between pupil and pupil are just as important as those between teacher and pupil. Teachers can play a significant part in the establishment of such relationships. One of the techniques we frequently use in our research is the identification of events that happen in classrooms and that seem to be indicative of the styles, preferences and effects of various teachers. Several hundred such critical events have been collected and analysed. In each case the observer records what led up to the event, what happened and what appeared to be the outcome. After the lesson, the teacher, and sometimes the pupils, were interviewed to elicit their view of what had transpired. One of the aspects of teaching highlighted in this way is how teachers set about establishing relationships between themselves and their pupils.

Consider the following account of science teacher Mr B in his second lesson with a class of newly inducted 11-year-olds, after a somewhat stern first lesson. He went on to establish a very positive relationship with the class and is generally liked and respected in the school with the reputation of being firm but fair. His pupils achieved good results in examinations. Note how he uses a skilful mixture of humour, self-deprecation, as well as a reminder that he too has a family, to change the mood to a more friendly, though still purposeful one.

I've got a son your age, and so when my wife and I were invited out to dinner the other night we tossed up to see who would stay at home babysitting, and of course I lost. I decided to watch football on television with my boy and the commentator began to use some very funny language – 'a square ball', 'the referee blew up', 'he left his foot behind' [laughter]. Well, we have some special language that we use in science that you will need to learn.

Activity 14

Use the 'critical events' approach to help you analyse the relationships in a classroom.

1   Find a fellow teacher or student who is willing to be observed. It is a useful paired activity, in which two students, or teachers, or a teacher and a student can observe each other's lessons.

2   During the lesson, look for something that happens that illustrates relationships between (a) teacher and pupil(s) and (b) pupil(s) and pupil(s). The events do not have to be spectacular: indeed, in most cases they will be ordinary everyday happenings, including, perhaps, a few words, a smile, a telling-off, some movement or some humour.

3   Fill in a pro-forma like the one opposite.

4   After the lesson, interview the teacher about the event, using a neutral opening like, 'Towards the beginning of the lesson you spoke to Rachel about her conversation with Alice. Can you tell me a bit about what happened?' You can then probe further with 'Why' questions or 'What do you think the effect was?' Avoid starting off with leading or tendentious questions such as, 'Why on earth did (or didn't) you …?' or 'Why were you so soft on Rachel and Alice … ?'

5   Interview pupils only if the teacher concerned and the head of the school agree. Talking to children about their classroom relationships with each other and/or their teacher is a sensitive matter, which must be handled in a thoroughly professional way. Student or inexperienced teachers should certainly ensure that they receive proper supervision for such an exercise.

6   See what generalisations and what specific points emerge from your classroom scrutiny. For example, it might seem, as a general conclusion, that the teacher has good relationships with the girls in the class, but less happy ones with the boys, or the other way round. A specific conclusion might be that the way a teacher handled a particular confrontation with a child who had misbehaved had been positive or negative.

7   Does anything need to be done to make relationships in this particular classroom better? What inferences, if any, can you draw about your own teaching?

Observation sheet – Personal relationships

A   What led up to the event?

B   What happened and who was involved?

C   What was the outcome?

D   Interview with teacher

E   Interview with pupil(s) (if agreed)

F   Conclusions

REWARDS AND PUNISHMENTS

Since teachers must act as a responsible parent does, society has to give them certain powers to exercise control or discharge the 'duty of care' which the law requires. Forms of punishment in particular in a school must be approved by the governors. This is to avoid, for example, children being kept in detention after school if this meant that they would miss their bus home to a remote rural area, or to a dangerous part of a city. Punishments are in fact governed by the law, which decrees that they must be 'reasonable', defined by one judge as:

- moderate
- not dictated by bad motives
- such as is usual in the school
- such as the parent of the child might expect it to receive if it had done wrong.

This certainly rules out racks and thumbscrews, and the 1986 Education Act made corporal punishment illegal in maintained schools. This ban applies not just to forms of corporal punishment, such as caning and hitting with a ruler, slipper or the hand, but also to a 'clip round the ear', which in any case was a potentially dangerous punishment.

Rewards are one of two principal kinds:

extrinsic   getting a star, a badge, a trophy, a prize, a privilege, something external, often visible, bestowed on behalf of the school or by the teacher.

intrinsic   satisfying one's curiosity, a glow of pride from a job well done, something coming more from within the individual.

Rewards and punishments can too readily be stereotyped as 'good' or 'bad'. For example, it would be easy to assume that rewards themselves are invariably positive and punishments are always negative. Yet a reward out of all proportion to whatever deed earned it, or a minor punishment that was fair and timely and, in retrospect, appreciated by the recipient as having had a positive effect, can soon reverse these simple labels. Similarly, it might be assumed that extrinsic rewards are crude bribes and that intrinsic rewards are the only things worth striving for, but some people need external recognition so that they can set their own standards for themselves. What is often much more important is the effect of rewards and punishments on the children concerned, whether the punishment was unfair, something greatly resented by children, or whether they had earned the reward for their own efforts.

Most rewards and punishments are unspectacular, often short-lived and taken for granted. This does not mean that they are of no importance. The two incidents below only occupied a few seconds, but they demonstrate that even a fleeting exchange can have a significant influence. The first shows a girl receiving praise for coping with her own embarrassment, the second describes a public shaming.

> The class has been making lists of the characteristics of the animals in *Animal Farm*. The teacher selects one person to read out her list. Amidst giggling, the girl complies. She appears embarrassed at having to stand up. When she has finished reading the teacher says, 'Well done, that was very good.' She smiles encouragement at the pupil who smiles back and sits down.

> The teacher states that she will not tolerate pupils talking when she is explaining something in her science lessons. She sees a girl talking as she says this, so she moves quickly over to her, puts her hands on the bench and stares into her face from close range. 'I will not tolerate [pause] talking at the same time.' At the teacher's speed of movement and shortening of the distance between her and the pupil the girl reddens and the class falls silent.

Look at the use of rewards and punishments in your school, remembering some of the more subtle ones like smiles, nods, using pupils' ideas, withholding attention or recognition, displaying children's work. Record some of these at both school and classroom level in the grid below. If you see more than one teacher, look for similarities and differences.

REWARDS	PUNISHMENTS
At school level	*At school level*
Public signs of reward – what does the school value? Pupils' work on display? Children made monitors? Academic success rewarded?	What is the school policy on punishment? What is permitted? Detention? Extra work? What is regarded as mild misbehaviour and what as more serious?
At classroom level	*At classroom level*
Look at teachers' use of rewards. Note the public ones but also smiles, nods, use of praise, encouragement.	Make notes about any punishments you see, either formal or less obvious. Look for sanctions such as loss of privilege, change of seat, sending out of class or to head, reprimands.

Unit 5 Skills, strategies and decision-making

Skilful teachers bring together a whole repertoire of related skills when they manage their classes effectively. These include the ability to prepare and plan; to choose or allow children to select topics and classwork that engage pupils and help them to learn; to use time and space effectively; to be vigilant and aware of what is happening in what may be a scattered, or unevenly shaped working area, as in labs, workshops and gymnasia; to make intelligent decisions in the light of context cues, often involving the rapid scanning of numerous messages; to handle deviancy and disruption; to establish good relationships and a set of rules and conventions that enhance orderly working and learning; to handle resources skilfully; to recognise and understand the wider constituency (including fellow teachers, the head, governors, parents, the local community) within which class management takes place.

Some of these skills have already been dealt with in this workbook, and those such as the management of lesson content are covered in other books in the series, on questioning and explaining, for example. Teaching skills need to be seen as a coherent whole rather than a discrete set of separate and unrelated competencies and techniques, and professional skills in a job like teaching can only be truly enhanced if teachers reflect on questions of value, asking 'Why?' as well as 'How?' or 'What?' In this unit we shall concentrate on the important matter of the effective management of time and space, as well as on some of the specific skills that need to be nurtured and developed when teachers make decisions in classrooms.

In Unit 1 we addressed the question of what constitutes skilful class management and what are your own perceptions and those of any group of colleagues, students or teachers with whom you work. Once you are clearer in your mind about your own beliefs and intentions, it is possible to consider certain specific aspects of class management in more detail. The cluster of related skills needed to manage a class of children in an effective manner includes the intelligent use of time and space.

MANAGING GROUPS AND INDIVIDUALS

One of the important strategic decisions teachers make about the management of time and space is whether to use whole class teaching, group work, individual assignments or a combination of these. Most teachers use a mixture of these approaches over a period of time, but some may not always make the best use of time and space for different activities, over- or under-using one form or another.

Let us suppose, for example, that an English teacher intends the class to make a mock local radio or television news programme. The pupils are to collect 'stories', as if they were reporters, and then compile a five-minute bulletin, video- or sound-record it, and finally play it back to the rest of the class. She might then make the following strategic decisions:

Whole class teaching   At the beginning of the lesson, to set the scene, ask about 'news', what it is, why events are newsworthy, how news programmes are assembled (important stories first, newsreader plus interviews or on-the-spot reporters, etc.). Then, to explain how the class will be split into news teams of five pupils, discuss how they might organise themselves, what they are to do, how they will record their bulletin. In the middle of the session, she might bring the whole class together to review what progress has been made, answer questions and solve problems. At the end, the whole class might listen to or watch each of the bulletins, discuss the choice of items, priorities, delivery, succinctness and information value.

Group work   After the beginning part of the lesson, groups of five work out their stories, discuss ideas, choose who should be reporters, who will actually read the news, who will do sound effects, pretend to be a member of the public being interviewed, etc.

Individual work   Digging out information, writing a short script for a 30-second item, practising using the video or cassette recorder, reading the bulletin.

You might like to make a list of possible circumstances in which whole class teaching, group work and individual assignments appear to make good sense, of what advantages and disadvantages each approach might offer teachers and pupils, and of the management concerns in each case. For example, you might speculate that during whole class teaching, control of behaviour might be easier if pupils are engaged, but harder if the more able and less able have lost interest; that it will take a great deal of effort to monitor effectively during individual assignment work; that managing groups doing different activities might involve more detailed preparation and extra mobility and vigilance. You can then test your own hypotheses against your experience in the classroom-based activities below and above.

THE MANAGEMENT OF TIME

In the context of classroom learning, the use of time is an important matter. There is often a limited amount of time available and skilful use of it can be the difference between children learning effectively and learning little. Teachers' sharing out of their own time – between planning and preparing, marking children's work, asking questions, giving information, listening to and talking with individuals or group, or taking part in extracurricular activities – is well worthy of scrutiny.

Anyone wishing to manage time effectively would find that some kind of occasional systematic analysis can be quite illuminating. Teaching is a busy job that requires all the energy that can be mustered for it, so this kind of analysis should not be overdone. For example, it is possible to attempt to record each hour a breakdown of how the previous hour has been spent. A series of headings can be assembled, such as 'planning and preparation', 'teaching children', 'attending formal or informal meetings', 'marking work' and 'assessing progress', 'social time' and the ubiquitous 'other'. Every hour the teacher can make a very quick and rough estimate of how many minutes were spent in each of the categories. It is then possible, at the end of a day or a week, to see how one's time has been spent.

Indeed, it is easy to be shocked at how much time has been devoted to meetings, how little time spent on teaching, or how much time assessment may take during certain periods of the school year. Though the exercise in itself consumes precious time, it is worth doing, on an occasional basis, especially when teachers are seeking to redirect their energies.

The main purpose of this section, however, is not to consider these broader issues, but rather to look specifically at time spent by children on the task in hand. The notion of 'time on task' is one that has received considerable attention during the last few years. One operational definition of the important concept of 'motivation' is 'the amount of time and the degree of arousal or attentiveness brought to a task or activity'.

Take as an example the game of chess. If you are not 'motivated' to play chess then you will give it little time or attention and probably, therefore, not play the game especially well. If, on the other hand, you are highly 'motivated', then you may well belong to a chess club, read books on chess, spend time on the chess column in your newspaper (rather than pass over it, as most readers do), perhaps even carry a pocket chess set around so that you can play through games you come across or play against other enthusiasts. In other words, you will devote a great deal of time in a psychologically aroused state to the game of chess and, as a result, you will probably be a better player than you would have been had you not been 'motivated'. The mere act of spending more time on something does not guarantee better learning, but it can certainly make a valuable contribution to it.

Time in itself, however, is an empty concept. If someone spent hours copying out telephone directories, then little of value would be learned. There are two highly significant features of time spent on the task that are essential requirements if effective learning is to take place. The first is that the time should be spent on something worthwhile, and the second is that there should be some degree of success by the pupil. If children were to spend a great deal of time, for example, writing down incorrect answers to arithmetical problems or constantly misspelling the same word, then they would actually be learning errors, and, once established, such errors are difficult to unlearn. Hence the need for careful scrutiny of the *kind* of activity that takes place, not merely of the *amount of time* spent on it.

In our research into secondary classrooms we have observed several hundred lessons during which we spent part of the time observing every single individual child in the class. One approach we used was to study each child for 20 seconds and then make two decisions. The first was to ask whether children appeared to be 'high' (14–20 seconds), 'medium' (7–13 seconds) or 'low' (0–6 seconds), in terms of on-task behaviour – that is, spending time on whatever they were supposed to be doing. The second was to record whether children were behaving well during that 20-second period, or were mildly or seriously 'deviant'. Mild deviance involved such matters as illicit chatter, movement, interfering with the work of another child. More serious deviance included physical aggression, vandalism, damage to property, or any behaviour significantly insulting to another child or the teacher.

In order to record these two pieces of information, researchers completed a grid as shown below. Supposing Mary had worked consistently and behaved well, John had worked for about half the twenty seconds and spent the rest distracting his neighbour and Alice had not appeared to be involved in the task at all and had called the teacher an 'old cow'. The resulting grid would have looked like the one below (though in real life it is not always so symmetrical, as pupils may be low on task but well behaved, for example).

Pupil	Seconds on task (out of 20)			Level of deviancy		
	Low (0–6)	Medium (7–13)	High (14–20)	None	Mild	More serious
1 Mary			✔	✔		
2 John		✔			✔	
3 Alice	✔					✔

Often it will seem crystal clear to the observer whether a pupil is engaged in the task or not and similarly whether or not a pupil is misbehaving, but on some occasions it will be unclear. It can be extremely difficult to decide whether someone who is staring intently into space is daydreaming or planning his next move, and, indeed, whether the daydreaming itself is an important part of learning, allowing someone a brief respite before the next intensive bout of work. Thus, any recordings of this kind are merely rough-and-ready estimates, valuable when taken into consideration alongside other evidence, but not in themselves flawless indicators of types of behaviour and successful learning.

Activity 16

You can use a data sheet like the one shown on page 57 to assemble a general picture of involvement in the task and misbehaviour in a class you observe. It is not usually possible to teach and conduct the exercise on your own class at the same time. The observer needs to be free to observe as accurately as possible and the teacher needs to be able to teach without the inhibition of having to record systematically. You will need to find someone able to observe your teaching, therefore, if you wish to have this sort of analysis of it. Unfortunately, too little time is made available for teachers to observe each other teach, but this is the sort of valuable exercise that can be done by two teachers working together on their own staff development programme, by two students in the same school for teaching practice, or by a student and a teacher sharing a class.

Method

Complete the data sheet on page 57, observing each pupil for twenty seconds and then, for each pupil, inserting one tick to indicate seconds on task and another to indicate level of deviancy. Study each pupil in the class and either do the exercise in a systematic manner, observing each area or section of the room in turn, or, if you know the pupils' names, in a random way, making sure you do not observe the same child twice. Make the best decision you can in each case. Also ensure the observations are done in a discreet and sensitive manner, from a suitable vantage point.

Calculate an involvement and a deviancy score for the lesson using the following procedure.

Involvement score (possible range 0–100)

First of all you must obtain Factor A. To do this you multiply the total number of pupils in the 'low' category by 0, the total number of pupils in the 'medium' category by 1 and the total in the 'high' category by 2; and add the resulting scores. Suppose you observe 28 pupils and find 2, 10 and 16 pupils to be 'low', 'medium' and 'high' on task respectively, then Factor A would be as follows:

'Low' on task	2 pupils	Multiplied by 0 = 0
'Medium' on task	10 pupils	Multiplied by 1 = 10
'High' on task	16 pupils	Multiplied by 2 = 32
Total	28 pupils	Factor A = 42 (i.e. 0 + 10 + 32)

Next, insert Factor A in the equation below:

$$\text{Involvement score} = \frac{\text{Factor A}}{\text{Total no of pupils} \times 2} = \frac{42}{28 \times 2} = \frac{42}{56} = 0.75$$

Finally multiply by 100, giving an involvement score of 75. If every child were fully involved the maximum score would be 100, and if no one were involved in the task the minimum score would be 0. The maximum of 100 would be obtained if all the pupils in the class were observed to be 'high' on task.

Deviancy score

Exactly the same procedure is adopted, but this time the 'none' category is multiplied by 0, the 'mild' is multiplied by 1 and the 'more serious' is multiplied by 2. Thus the following distribution would produce a deviancy score of 20 if there were 25 pupils in the class, with 16, 8 and 1 pupils in the 'none', 'mild' and 'more serious' categories respectively.

'None'	6 pupils	multiplied by 0 = 0
'Mild'	8 pupils	multiplied by 1 = 8
'More serious'	1 pupil	multiplied by 2 = 2
Total	25 pupils	Factor A = 10 (i.e. 0 + 8 + 2)

$$\text{Deviancy score} = \frac{\text{Factor A}}{\text{Total no of pupils} \times 2} = \frac{10}{25 \times 2} = \frac{10}{50} = 0.20$$

This score of 0.20 multiplied by 100 then gives a deviancy score of 20.

Discussion of the observation between the teacher and the observer of Activity 16 can cover such points as:

- What is the general level of involvement and why is the picture as it is?
- What is the general level of good behaviour/misbehaviour and what sort of misbehaviour takes place?
- Which children behave in what manner? Give attention to each child if possible, not just to those who misbehave or work intensively.
- Is the observed behaviour typical (it is wise to do more than one such observation with a class).
- Discuss some of the events the observer witnessed, both positive and negative kinds.
- Observations can be compiled by the recording of critical events (see Activity 14).

Consider ways of increasing involvement and reducing misbehaviour. This involves addressing such matters as:

- Was/were the assignment(s) suitable and worthwhile?
- Had the ground been prepared sufficiently, so that pupils were clear what they had to do?
- Was the teacher's use of his/her own time effectively managed or was the setting up and/or development of the lesson too protracted, slow, or tedious?
- Did the teacher monitor pupils' work and behaviour?
- Was misbehaviour handled effectively and was good behaviour properly acknowledged?
- What happened when pupils finished their work?
- Were pupils able to work independently if this was what was required, or were they too reliant on the teacher?
- Was the achievement of individual children satisfactory given the time available? (It is sometimes worth choosing six 'target' pupils, three boys and three girls, a boy and a girl from among each of high, medium and low ability pupils, and looking specifically at what they achieved during the observation period.)

In an observation period it is sometimes possible to conduct more than one such 'circuit' of the class. If this is done, then involvement and deviancy levels can be calculated for different kinds of activity. Questions to be asked include:

- Were there significant-looking differences in pattern for different kinds of activity?
- What kinds of activity secured highest involvement and lowest misbehaviour?
- Was there more misbehaviour when certain things happened? (For example, it sometimes happens that deviancy increases during transitions from one activity to another, especially if movement and jostling occur.)
- Were there significant differences?

As a result, the teacher and observer can discuss any difficult moments and find ways of managing future potential problems more effectively.

INDIVIDUAL PUPIL OBSERVATION

Teacher: . . . . Date: . . . . Lesson: . . . .

Pupil	Seconds on task (out of 20)			Level of deviancy		
	Low 0–6	Medium 7–13	High 14–20	None	Mild	More serious
1						
2						
3						
4						
5						
6						
7						
8						
9						
10						
11						
12						
13						
14						
15						
16						
17						
18						
19						
20						
21						
22						
23						
24						
25						
26						

	× 0	× 1	× 2	× 0	× 1	× 2
27						
28						
29						
30						
31						
32						
33						
34						
35						
Total						
	× 0	× 1	× 2	× 0	× 1	× 2
Factor A	0			0		
	Sum					

Formula $\dfrac{\text{Sum of Factor A}}{\text{Total of pupils} \times 2} \times 100 = \text{Involvement or deviancy level}$

Task involvement level . . . .

Deviancy level . . . .

During research projects we have observed hundreds of lessons using this approach. There was considerable variety in the scores obtained and in the critical events analysed. A summary of some averages of over two hundred lessons given by a group of experienced teachers in one study is shown below.

	Involvement score	Deviancy score
Average of whole group	71	5
Lowest average for any individual teacher	38	0
Lowest score for any individual lesson	28	0
Highest average for any individual teacher	92	20
Highest score for any individual lesson	100	26

Great caution must be exercised when comparing scores with these group figures. Involvement and deviancy scores are not measures of *quality*. They are rough-and-ready estimates of *attentiveness to the task*. It would be possible to obtain a high involvement and low deviancy score by terrorising pupils into copying out telephone directories, but the educational value would be zero.

Some of the above figures represent lessons with small orderly classes, and others represent lessons with large classes in inner-city schools working with extremely difficult pupils. Qualitative elements, such as the nature of the group, the size of the class, the available materials, equipment, furnishings and extra adult ancillary help, all affect behaviour and concentration. Other aspects, such as the amount of time teachers allow between asking a question and a pupil's answering, are dealt with elsewhere in this series, for example, in the volumes on questioning and explaining.

THE MANAGEMENT OF SPACE

The physical environment for learning can be very important, so it is equally illuminating to study the use of space in a school, to see how wisely it is being used. Freiberg (1999b) describes the case of a school in which several fights broke out each day each day around the dining hall. When he looked at the environment he found there was a large amount of noise and chaos in the space where these fights took place: the rattle of metal knives and forks, the noise from the kitchen, the clatter of plates being cleared. All these factors led to voices being raised, so everyone seemed to be shouting and jostling, producing a high degree of stress. The school took several steps to reduce noise, appointed pupil monitors to help with supervision and the atmosphere became that of a civilised restaurant. The fights gradually disappeared.

Consider the following two examples.

Example 1   Art lesson

A class of 13-year-olds is engaged in painting in an art room. From time to time there is disruption in two different areas. One is by the sink, when pupils go to wash their hands or their brushes and those working in the area complain about being jostled ('Please, miss, make them go round'). The other is next to a cupboard that contains books and pictures of various kinds which some pupils consult. Again, those in the proximity of the cupboard complain that they are nudged whenever the cupboard doors are opened.

Example 2   Whole class explanation and demonstration

In a design and technology workshop the teacher is demonstrating how to use a certain type of hammer without breaking the object on which it is being used. As he demonstrates the technique, some pupils crane their necks to see what he is doing, others peer round their computer, although they are engaged in a different task, while a few clamber over their fellows, amid protests, to secure a better vantage point.

In both these examples it was the ineffective use of space that led to problems. In the first one, failure to clear a space for pupils to get to and from the sink, and the siting of the book and resources cupboard, produced friction between pupils working near the facilities and those seeking access to them. Movement and transitions from one activity to another often spark physical contact and confrontation, so the potential for aggravation should be minimised. In the second example, working at computers or tables was fine for most of the class's activities, but when they had to listen to the teacher explaining to the whole group, some kind of modification was needed so that all could see properly.

Many teachers work in classrooms that are less than ideal, so the best has to be made of what is available. However, it is worth thinking carefully about how to use the space at your disposal. In our own home, we may, if we are lucky, be able to spend a great deal of time designing a kitchen, deciding exactly where the cooker and washing machine should go, whether one can squeeze in a dining corner, and thinking about the activities that will take place and how they can best be accommodated. Time spent planning an effective classroom layout, given the amount of time spent there, will be a wise investment.

Activity 17

Using a piece of squared paper, design a classroom layout with a particular class in mind: it might be one you are currently teaching, have recently taught or one you imagine you might have to teach in future. You should make the following assumptions:

- You have about 52 square metres (m^2) available.
- There will be anything from 24 to 32 pupils present at any one time.
- A pupil sitting at a single desk or table would need about 1–1.25 m^2 of floor space.
- Six children sitting round a bench or table would need 4–5 m^2.
- Three pupils at a rectangular or semi-hexagonal table would need about 2–2.5 m^2.
- You will need at least 2 m^2 of teacher's storage space.
- Each square on your plan represents 1 m^2.

You might, therefore, draw a plan of a rectangle or an L-shape (circular, oval or star-shaped rooms sound interesting, but architects usually quote astronomical building costs for less conventional shapes).

Some parts of schools may be designed in a more open-plan manner, with paired classrooms and shared specialist areas. If you wish to design something along these lines, then simply assume that part or all of the walls could be removed so you could simply design your own home base part of the unit. Next, you should draw into the squared paper your layout showing where pupils would sit and work, what sort of facilities you would like and where these might be located. When you have completed your sketch, make a list of what resources and facilities you would like to see in an adjacent additional 10 m^2 per class of shared resource area, available to each teacher.

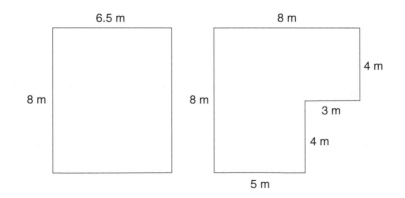

You can look critically at your plan and see if it fits your preferred ways of working as effectively as possible. For example, will it allow:

- maximum ease of movement when required for yourself and the class;
- pupils to work together or alone in a variety of assignments;
- you to address the whole class when necessary;
- proper display of work;
- flexibility to vary activities from day to day or lesson to lesson, with minimum disruption.

In addition, you can try to identify possible problems of management: for example, where excessive and difficult movement might occur as people walk over to some facility they need; whether you would be able to see all that went on, or if there might be blind spots; how you would deal with pupils working in the working shared-resource area (e.g. what the rules would be, whether permission would be required to go there, or if they would have to report back, how you would keep in touch with what was happening in the area).

Finally, you can consider how close you can make your own classroom to your 'ideal' working area, whether the layout of your room enhances or hinders pupil learning and whether the best use is being made of floor space.

VIGILANCE

Knowing what individuals and groups are doing, anticipating problems before they occur, spotting someone who appears bewildered and needs help, all these are examples of the need for vigilance. In order to see what is happening in what may sometimes be a large or irregularly shaped area, skilful teachers develop what Jacob Kounin called 'withitness' – that is, the ability to split your attention between the individual or group you are with and the rest of the class, to 'have eyes in the back of your head'.

This involves two kinds of use of the eyes:

- the first is the ability to engage pupils in *eye contact*, in other words to use your own eyes to look at theirs, for eyes are most important for giving as well as receiving messages;
- the second is to be able to *sweep* the classroom rapidly to take in what is happening in various parts of the working area.

Exactly the same applies outside the classroom, in a hall or outdoors, for example, and can be vital for such matters as safety especially on a field trip or during a swimming lesson. In order to see the workings of this process of scanning and eye contact, it is necessary to understand how the human eye works. The figure overleaf shows three angles, as seen by our eyes. Only a very small area, about two to three degrees, is seen in very sharp focus, but we have *awareness* of nearly 180 degrees. As a result, when a teacher looks across a classroom, a V-shaped wedge of about 30 to 45 degrees is in reasonably sharp focus.

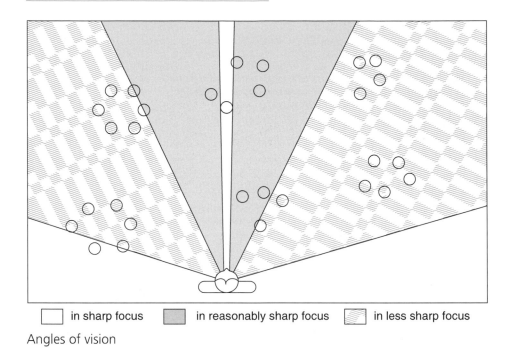

| | in sharp focus | | in reasonably sharp focus | | in less sharp focus |

Angles of vision

The effect of this is shown in the two pictures opposite. In picture A, small zones are highlighted. This shows approximately the area that is in very sharp focus when a teacher looks across a room: it may be a single face, a picture, a clock, but the actual area is quite small. Picture B, on the other hand, shows the three zones together, a central 2 to 3 degrees are in very sharp focus, a 45-degree area in reasonably sharp focus and the rest of the 170- to 180-degree zone in more fuzzy 'awareness' form.

The result of all this is quite clear, especially where classroom interaction is concerned. For example, it has often been observed that teachers' questions may be largely directed into that V-shaped 45-degree wedge in front of them. Thus teachers who always teach from near their desk or at the blackboard may find that most of their questions are addressed to or answered by children in central positions, and that those sitting near the edge of the room are less frequently involved. Since children understand perfectly well the dynamics of classroom life, those who want to be in the 'busy traffic' area often head for seats or tables in central locations, those seeking a quieter environment may choose the periphery and seats or tables by walls and windows, and it is not unknown for those who disrupt to choose the corners furthest away from the teacher's desk.

Vigilance is not, however, something that should be undertaken in isolation. There are many common situations in which vigilance and effective use of eyes can pay off, like the following:

Picture A

Picture B

Anticipating problems

The teacher notices that pupils in one part of the room have finished their task early and are beginning to distract others.

Anticipating problems

Monitoring work

Walking round the class involves more than just creating a draught. Teachers who monitor children's work effectively during class time have a clear picture about children's learning.

Monitoring work

Public audit

'Jason, how are you getting on? You should all be nearly done now, we've got about seven minutes left.' An occasional audit signals that the teacher knows what is happening, but if it occurs too frequently, then it might become a barrier to concentration.

Public audit

Avoiding accidents

Design and technology sessions can be absorbing and exciting, but safety is an important matter as well.

Avoiding accidents

Personal and social education

Are children helping each other, sharing, waiting their turn, or are they behaving negatively belittling each other, showing meanness?

Personal and social education

CONTEXT CUES

Trainee teachers sometimes ask, 'What do you do if ..?' questions, and are then disappointed when teachers or tutors reply, 'It depends on the circumstances.' Teaching would be a much easier occupation if all events within certain categories were identical. Yet classrooms are unlike factory production lines where robots can insert rivets in precisely the same place, with precisely the same effect, for week upon week.

Activity 18   Incident

A student teacher, new to her school, suddenly finds Gareth, a 14-year-old pupil from another class, walking into her lesson, and crossing the room between herself and a group of pupils she is addressing. She is a little taken aback at the intrusion of this stranger, and is not certain how to react.

1   Consider just a few of the countless possible context factors, of which she might or might not be aware, and reflect on how each might affect her reaction.

(a)   The school is open plan and freedom of movement is permitted, even encouraged.

(b)   Gareth is known as a regular trouble-maker who goes to other parts of the school and causes disruption.

(c)   Gareth's father is seriously ill in hospital and so he is upset, not behaving normally.

(d)   The head has sent Gareth round the school with a message.

(e)   Gareth is very tall for his age.

(f)   Gareth is very small for his age.

(g)   The teacher and children are working with potentially dangerous technology equipment.

(h)   The class laughs uproariously.

(i)   The class goes completely silent.

(j)   Gareth is a pupil who has been statemented as having learning difficulties and easily becoming confused.

2   Think of other context cues that might influence a teacher's decision and discuss how, in each case, the teacher's reaction to the incident could or should be affected.

DEVIANCY AND DISRUPTION

Definitions of 'deviancy' vary considerably. If you have completed Activity 16 (see pages 55–8) and observed individual pupils one by one, you will have made your own subjective judgements about different kinds of deviancy or disruption. For some teachers, any kind of talking to another pupil might constitute naughty or deviant behaviour; for others, talk might be permitted only provided it is related to the task in hand; yet others might tolerate quite a high level of social chat.

Our studies of both primary and secondary classrooms have shown that most misbehaviour was of a minor, if irritating, kind primarily related to over-noisy talk. In one study of more than two hundred lessons given by student teachers in secondary schools (Wragg, 1989), the most common source of deviant behaviour was indeed excessively noisy or irrelevant talk, followed by distraction of others, unsuitable use of materials or equipment, eating in class and illicit movement (leaving seat without permission, running). In about three-quarters of cases, the student teachers made some response before the deviance escalated, most commonly an order to cease, a reprimand, or a statement of rule. More serious matters, like physical aggression to another pupil and insults to the teacher, were only recorded in one or two per cent of the lesson segments analysed. Studies of experienced teachers in both primary and secondary schools have also shown noisy chatter to be the most common form of misbehaviour and serious misbehaviour to be relatively rare (Wragg, 1993).

The Elton Report (DES, 1989), a government-sponsored enquiry into discipline in schools, reported questionnaire responses that were very similar to our lesson observations. A survey by Sheffield University for the Elton Committee found that primary teachers reported children talking noisily or out of turn, distracting others, and inappropriate use of materials, as the most frequent occurrences they had to deal with. The Elton Report concluded:

Our recommendations relate to a whole range of discipline problems, particularly persistent disruption. We found that most schools are on the whole well ordered. But even in well-run schools minor disruption appears to be a problem. The relatively trivial incidents which most concern teachers make it harder for teachers to teach and pupils to learn.

Nevertheless, even though relatively little serious misbehaviour has been noted in live studies of classrooms, there are two important matters that need to be addressed. The first is what to do about such matters as noise levels, the second is how to handle the more serious forms of misbehaviour when they occur. Countries like the United Kingdom and Australia (Slee, 1999) have both reported increases in the use of exclusions as a sanction, some writers ascribing this to the spread of free market policies to education which sets schools in competition with each other (Ball, 1994). Parsons and Castle (1998) estimated the cost of permanent exclusions to be £81m per year, two-thirds of this being the costs of replacement teaching for those excluded.

Activity 19

We put a number of discipline situations to teachers in the form of photographs, some illustrating a more serious problem.

1   Consider the two pictures A and B and the storylines that go with them. Picture A shows two children pushing each other, Picture B a confrontation with a girl pupil.

2   Decide in each case what you would do if this happened in your own class.

3   Consider and discuss the responses of teachers in interview. The replies are given in descending order of frequency so that the first answer is the one most often given.

Picture A

1   Separate the two children.
2   Find out what has happened.
3   It would depend on the children/their expectations/school sanctions.
4   Look at the task the children are supposed to be doing and reassess it and the situation.
5   Tell them off/comment on their behaviour.
6   See it as time wasting and so get them back to work.
7   Punish them (most frequent suggestion – keep them in).
Other mentions – get them to sit next to the teacher, bring them out, talk individually to them.

Picture B

1   Speak to her on her own, now or later.
2   Show emotion – anger, sorrow, upset, humour.
3   It would depend on the child.
4   Send to the head.
5   Involve the whole class in some way.
6   Punish the girl.
7   Ask her to repeat it.
8   Tell her off.
Other mentions – withdraw her, get her to rub out the scribbling.

Picture A – Messing about

Picture A   You're sitting with your back to this group when you hear a noise. You turn around and see two children messing about. You have told them off once that day for not getting on with their work. What, if anything, do you do?

Picture B – 'Old cow'

Picture B   You have caught this girl scribbling on someone else's book. You have told her off in front of the class and you hear her mutter 'old cow' under her breath. The children nearby snigger. What if anything, do you do?

4   Discuss how teachers should deal with more serious examples of misbehaviour. Consider the following:

(a)   Seeing a child on his/her own after the lesson or at break and consider what safeguards might be needed for both the teacher and the child (e.g. overawing young child, need for a witness).

(b)   When parents would need to be involved (when does a routine matter become more serious, for example, or what constitutes behaviour so unacceptable, or so worrying, that parents must be involved).

(c)   When governors, particularly the chairman, should be involved, for example, in the case of a pupil being excluded. Remember that governors have responsibility for discipline in the school, even if it is the head and teachers who are responsible for the day-to-day handling of discipline matters. There have been assertions that some schools might have excluded pupils too readily, that exclusions should be used sparingly and also that primary boys are about fifteen times more likely to be excluded than primary girls. Also some parents and community groups have complained that too many African-Caribbean boys have been excluded, a matter into which the City of Birmingham, for example, conducted an enquiry. Australian evidence (Slee, 1995) has been similar (four times as many boys as girls excluded, more likely suspension of Aboriginal children).

(d)   What use might be made of any special facilities available inside or outside the school, such as a special unit for disruptive pupils (often named 'sin bins' by the press, not the most positive label), or the help of an educational psychologist.

(e)   What 'low key' methods can be used inside the school, like the use of 'time out' (a spell outside the class, say, with the head or another teacher, possibly in a 'sanctuary', a classroom specially equipped for the purpose).

(f)   Whether the misbehaving pupil is being overwhelmed by several adults, perhaps responding in contradictory ways.

Unit 6 Developing and enhancing competence

A WHOLE SCHOOL APPROACH

One of the features of the many initiatives to improve practice is the stress now-adays on the 'dynamic school', within which all teachers try to change judiciously what they do for the better (Wragg, 1999), so collectively benefiting the whole effort. There has also been emphasis on improving what a school achieves by working from the classroom upwards, instead of relying on a model from outside, or one imposed solely from above (Stoll and Fink, 1992). It is especially valuable if all the teachers in the same school discuss their class management strategies and experiences, not with a view to becoming clones of each other, but so that the kinds of inconsistencies that may confuse pupils, or cause problems, can be considered openly.

Frances Farrer (2000) describes how a whole school decided to spend time discussing some of the key values and beliefs that underpinned life in a civilised community, such as honesty, trust, friendship, respect, tolerance. Younger and older pupils, teachers, parents, support staff and external contacts like police officers, were all involved and invited to act positively for the benefit of the whole community. This was done in a primary school, but a similar approach can work in a secondary school, if there is a collective will.

As in the case described by Farrer there are also roles for the whole community. Teachers need to consider how they manage time, resources and space, what sort of rules and relationships have been established in their classes or what to do about disorderly behaviour; but so too do children, for they need to learn to take responsibility, make decisions, organise themselves effectively, control their own behaviour. Furthermore, parents need to be included in the process, and governors, since they are responsible for staff appointments and for school policy. Classroom assistants, lunchtime supervisors and ancillaries need to be aware of school policy also, and rules and conventions should apply in the playground, dining areas, circulation space and cloakrooms, not just in classrooms, although there may be some differences.

A consistent whole school policy is essential

One way of raising issues is to begin with consideration of hypothetical events rather than those that have actually happened within the school. It is sometimes easier to do this without prejudice, recrimination or blame being attached. For example, take the case of bullying, something that can happen quite suddenly even in the best-run school. If teachers begin by reviewing a case that has *actually* happened, within recent memory, in their own school, then the head and teacher concerned may feel defensive, as if their actions are coming under close scrutiny, and it may be difficult to discuss policy separately from personalities. Activity 20 is based on an actual letter sent by a parent to the head of a school.

Activity 20

1   Consider this letter, which was written by the parent of a boy to his head teacher.

Dear Mr X,

I have thought long and hard before writing this letter, but I should like to come and see you about my son Michael who is being bullied regularly by two boys in his class. The reason I have not contacted you before is because Michael has begged me not to say anything, as he does not want to make things worse, and he is frightened that one of the boys in particular will take revenge on him.

The two boys are Ian Jenkins and Andrew Wilson, and Ian Jenkins is much worse than Andrew. In lessons they often tease Michael. Ian Jenkins hid his ruler the other day and Andrew Wilson wrote on his new bag. It is usually petty things in the classroom, but outside is much worse. They often pick on him in the yard at playtime and that is why he has started coming home for lunch. They have told him that they are going to 'get him' after school, and one night they chased him down the whole length of Brook Street and he had to run all the way home. I know it sounds silly, but he was terrified when Ian Jenkins said he was going to get a big knife and cut his liver out.

Yesterday was the final straw. Michael came home and told me that Ian Jenkins wanted him to give him 50p or he would beat him up. That is why I have kept Michael at home today. I should like to come and see you as soon as possible, but please do not say anything to the two boys. I dare not tell Michael I have written to you and when I come to see you I shall have to tell him I am going shopping and leave him at his grandma's.

Yours sincerely

Mrs Elizabeth Gray

2   Consider how the head should react to this letter. In particular consider:

Confidentiality   Mrs Gray asks for confidentiality. Should the head persuade her to let him or the boy's form tutor talk discreetly with the boys concerned?

Form tutor   What should the form tutor and others who teach the class do about events said to be happening in the classroom?

Playground   What should be done about events said to be happening in the school grounds?

After school   What should be done about events that happen after school? (Teachers are legally *in loco parentis* while children are on their journey to or from school.)

Parents   Assume that eventually Mrs Gray agrees that the matter may be raised in a discreet way. Should the head see the parents of Ian Jenkins and Andrew Wilson? If not, why not? If yes, for what purpose?

Pupils   What should the head and class teacher do about the other pupils involved? What should the head and the class teacher each do? Should they be interviewed separately or together? How should each one's version of events be elicited? What action should be taken if Michael's version of the story is (a) untrue? (b) partly true, but exaggerated? (c) entirely true?

3   Discuss what might be done in your own school to prevent bullying and whether the school's code of practice needs amendment.

This activity can also be done in a modified form by governors (they can see and discuss Mrs Gray's letters at a governors' meeting or training conference and consider or review school policy in the light of their discussion) or by parents. If parent groups consider the letter, it is important that they not only imagine they are the parents of Michael Gray, but also the parents of Ian Jenkins. If you are the parent of Michael Gray you may well want immediate retribution and punishment, but if you are the parent of Ian Jenkins you will ask about such matters as whether Michael Gray is telling the truth, whether he has himself been a pest to your son or needled him in some way and whether he exaggerates or fantasises about events. There are often several aspects and versions of such a story, and it is important to hear them.

Bullying, however, is a serious matter and should always be investigated. My own reaction to the Michael Gray story, if his account turned out to be true, would be to see his parents first; persuade them to let me investigate discreetly with the class teacher and also to talk to Michael; next to talk to Ian and Andrew, first separately and then together; subsequently to confer again with the class teacher to compare all versions of events; to see the parents of Ian and Andrew, not just about the bullying but also about the extortion; to take whatever action then seemed necessary in the light of interviews and discussions; finally to raise the issue of bullying with other children in the school, some time later and in the context of a made-up story about some children in a school in another country and in the context of 'treating other people as you would like to be treated yourself'. It is most important, however, in any guidelines, to make provision to hear different accounts of events. Simply to decide prematurely and without any evidence that the alleged bully is a villain who should be punished, or the alleged victim is a wimp who should be toughened up, is to court disaster.

The question of bullying is an emotive one, but the case study approach can be used to discuss other matters of importance to class management in the school. It is not difficult to invent hypothetical storylines based on real events and then discuss individual and group policy. Here are just four possibilities. It is important to start with a fictional version so that individuals feel less under the microscope.

1   *Punishment*   Mrs Jones keeps people in at lunchtime if they come into her classroom without permission at break. In the room next door, however, Mr Brown does not mind children coming in, so long as they do not mess about. What do you do if teachers' punishment conventions vary? Review the use of punishments in the school.

2   *Rewards*   Mrs Thomas gives points and commendations for good work. Mr Jackson teaches the same subject to a parallel class in the same year, so his class asks if they can have them. Mr Jackson replies that he does not want to operate that sort of system as children should learn to enjoy doing their work for its own sake. Does it matter if individual teachers have different reward systems?

3   *Resources*   The school's bill for paper and card is increasing. Mr Smith says that the trouble is that some of the newer teachers waste paper, and that when he was at school he learned the importance of using paper sparingly, because there was not much about. Some of the younger teachers say that they do not 'waste' paper and materials, but if you want children to fulfil the sort of curriculum requirements that speak of 'improving a design' or 'redrafting a text', then you are bound to give pupils a second or third opportunity to better their first effort. Should anything be done?

4   *Noise*   Miss Carter and Mr Jessop are in adjacent classrooms with only a sliding partition between them, which is sometimes open and sometimes closed. The problem is that Miss Carter's area is usually quiet and Mr Jessop's much noisier, with more movement and the babble of voices and scrapping of chairs. Friction between the teachers begins to grow. Should anything be done about it? If not, why not? If yes, who should do what?

TEACHER APPRAISAL AND STAFF DEVELOPMENT

In a large-scale study of teacher appraisal (Wragg *et al.*, 1996) we found that only half of the teachers studied said that they had changed what they did in the classroom as a result of being appraised. If appraisal is supposed to lead to improvement, then this figure seems low, as one would expect all teachers to have changed, since no one is perfect. There are numerous ways in which work on class management can be incorporated into both staff development and teacher appraisal programmes, for the two should be related, appraisal without development being a somewhat arid and pointless procedure. Among possibilities are the use of some of the activities in this book, most of which can be translated into action with very little extra resources other than time, some elementary organisation and goodwill. Other options include the following:

Microteaching modified

The set of techniques known as 'microteaching' was developed originally at Stanford University. In its early form, small groups of children were taught for five or ten minutes with the teacher concentrating on some particular skill, like 'questioning' or 'explaining'. The teacher was video-taped with a small group of pupils, the lesson was then analysed, and then the teacher was able to try again with a similar group of children in the light of this analysis and feedback. The problem with microteaching when it was first developed was that it was very labour-intensive, useful for trainees in a college, but less manageable with experienced teachers in a school. In any case, using microteaching for the development of class management skills needs bigger groups of children, say at least twelve and possibly a half or even a full class.

Difficult, though more manageable, is a variation of the original format. The teacher can decide on some particular aspect of class management, like 'managing interactions', 'handling group work', or 'monitoring progress' and then be videoed with a class. Afterwards, the teacher studies the video with an appraiser, a colleague, or a tutor, discussing aspects of class management that seem important. On a subsequent occasion, preferably as soon afterwards as possible, the teacher is videoed again with the same class, this time trying to modify practice in the light of feedback.

Film, television and video

There are several films such as *Blackboard Jungle* or *To Sir with Love*, and television series like *Grange Hill*, where a teacher is shown having discipline problems. Although some of the filmed manifestations are not close to real life, there are sometimes particular scenes in certain films that do capture the flavour of a lesson going amiss. Teachers could make their own video with a class, role-playing scenes of misbehaviour in classrooms. Those scenes can be shown and discussed with colleagues.

Interactive technology

The development of highly interactive forms of technology, with speedy access to high quality film, can be very useful. Although there is often a shortage of good filmed material in each of the subjects taught in secondary schools, the facility to call up scenes of classroom life, look at and discuss them, and then bring on screen further scenes showing the outcomes of the events shown earlier has numerous fruitful possibilities.

Pictures and slides

There are several pictures in this book and it is not difficult to take one's own photographs of scenes from classroom life, real or role-played. A still picture is sometimes easier to discuss than moving film.

Literature

There are several accounts of classroom life in novels such as Thomas Mann's *Buddenbrooks* (a class destroying the teacher during registration and roll call), James Joyce's *A Portrait of the Artist as a Young Man* (the prefect of studies flogging pupils for idleness), or Tolstoy's *Yasnaya Polyana* (the silence and orderliness in the lessons of a teacher from a German seminary). Some writers capture the flavour of a lesson more skilfully than any social science textbook, and literary extracts can make excellent discussion material.

Paired learning

One of the most effective ways of improving teachers' or students' professional skills is for them to work in pairs, each taking a turn observing the other teach. Several activities in this book lend themselves to this approach. For example, the teacher observing can note the behaviour of, say, six target pupils and then feed this back to the person teaching, who in turn can do the same for the first teacher. If the focus is on 'vigilance', 'time spent on the task', or 'personal relationships', not only are valuable pieces of information learned by the observer, but feeding these back to the teacher, who can then reflect and act on practice and professional skill, can lead to a real improvement in class management competence.

Paired work of this kind should take place during appraisal, but unfortunately the observation of one person by another in schools is too often seen as hierarchical, a superior dissecting a subordinate, rather than collegial, two people working co-equally to improve both their classroom practice. For effective staff development there is no reason why the superior–subordinate stereotype should not be broken.

A COHERENT VIEW

One very useful exercise for both teachers and student teachers is to set class management firmly into the context of reflection and action across the whole repertoire of teaching skills. On its own, the ability to manage people, resources, time or space is meaningless. Only in a context will techniques and insights acquire value and meaning. This means that class management needs to be seen alongside the other skills that teachers develop, such as the ability to explain new concepts clearly, to ask different kinds of questions or to listen attentively to what children are saying. These skills are covered in other books in the series.

Professional skills should not be dismembered into components that are too small. It is quite right to focus on something broad and generic, such as 'class management', or a particular aspect of it, like 'vigilance', but it is foolish to dismantle teaching into hundreds of tiny molecular particles, minute individual competencies, such as 'can hold stick of chalk in right hand', and even more unwise to try to teach competence in this discrete, atomised form.

It is worthwhile for student teachers and for experienced teachers in a school to spend some time thinking about the nature of the professional skills they seek to develop in themselves and their colleagues. This may involve many different forms of reflection and action, for professional competence is really made up of clusters of intelligent thoughts that are translated into intelligent action. One useful staff development approach is to devise a set of headings and sub-headings and consider these. It may be in some hierarchical form, with lower levels and higher levels that can be reached by more proficient teachers.

In class management, for example, a notion like 'organise the handing out and collection of materials' might be a fairly basic matter; involving a teacher thinking about how this can best be organised. Indeed, pupils themselves could work it out. On the other hand, 'judging the right language register, appropriate response to and suitable activities for a pupil bewildered by a new mathematical or scientific concept' clearly exerts a much higher level of intellectual and practical demand.

There have been many attempts to construct hierarchies of skills, separating elementary versions of them from what are arguably more advanced levels. Topics can include such matters as 'managing whole class interactive teaching', 'monitoring individual and group work', 'management of order', 'planning and preparation'.

The problem with a hierarchical view is that, by the time we reach the demands of the highest level, the requirements are such that even the most gifted teachers may turn pale, and all of us feel guilty that we do not attain them. Nonetheless, such a mapping exercise does at least clarify people's aspirations. It is far more effective if a group of people work out a set of precepts to which they feel committed personally and professionally, than if such a set is merely given to them by somebody else.

References

Ball, S.J. (1994) *Education Reform*, Buckingham: Open University Press.

Bantock, G.H. (1965) *Freedom and Authority in Education*, London: Faber and Faber.

DES (1989) *Discipline in Schools*, The Elton Report, London: HMSO.

Farrer, F. (2000) *A Quiet Revolution*, London: Rider.

Freiberg, H.J. (1999a) *Beyond Behaviorism: Changing the Classroom Management Paradigm*, Boston: Allyn and Bacon.

Freiberg, H.J. (ed.) (1999b) *School Climate*, London: Falmer Press.

Gage, N.L. (1978) *The Scientific Basis of the Art of Teaching*, New York: Teachers College Press.

—— (1985) *Hard Gains in the Soft Sciences*, Bloomington, Ill.: Phi Delta Kappa.

Gillborn, D. and Youdell, D. (2000) *Rationing Education*, Buckingham: Open University Press.

Glasser, W. (1969) *Schools without Failure*, New York: Harper and Row.

Kelly, G.A. (1970) 'A brief introduction to personal construct theory', in D. Bannister (ed.) *New Perspectives in Personal Construct Theory*, London: Academic Press.

Kounin, J.S. (1970) *Discipline and Group Management in Classrooms*, New York: Holt, Rinehart and Winston.

Kyriacou, C. (1997) *Effective Teaching in Schools*, Cheltenham: Stanley Thornes.

Miller, A. (1996) *Pupil Behaviour and Teacher Culture*, London: Cassell.

Neill, A.S. (1962) *Summerhill*, London: Victor Gollancz.

Parsons, C. and Castle, F. (1998) 'The cost of school exclusion in England', *International Journal of Inclusive Education*, 2(4): 277–294.

Rogers, C.R. and Freiberg, H.J. (1994) *Freedom to Learn*, New York: Macmillan.

Skinner, B.F. (1968) *The Technology of Teaching*, New York: Appleton-Century-Crofts.

Slee, R. (1995) *Changing Theories and Practices of School Discipline*, London: Falmer Press.

—— (1999) 'Folk Devils and the Morality of the Panics over Classroom Discipline', Paper presented at the American Educational Research Association Annual Conference, Montreal, April 1999.

Stoll, L. and Fink, D. (1992) 'Effecting school change – the Halton approach', *School Effectiveness and School Improvement*, 3(1): 19–38.

Wang, M.C., Haertel, G.D. and Walberg, H.J. (1993) 'Towards a knowledge base for school learning', *Review of Educational Research*, 63(3): 249–294.

Wragg, E.C. (ed.) (1989) *Classroom Teaching Skills*, London: Routledge.

Wragg, E.C. (1993) *Primary Teaching Skills*, London: Routledge.

Wragg, E.C., Wikeley, F., Wragg, C.M. and Haynes, G.S. (1996) *Teacher Appraisal Observed*, London: Routledge.

Wragg, E.C. (1997) *The Cubic Curriculum*, London: Routledge.

—— (1999) *An Introduction to Classroom Observation*, second edition, London: Routledge.

Wragg, E.C., Haynes, G.S., Wragg, C.M. and Chamberlin, R.P. (2000) *Failing Teachers?*, London: Routledge.

Learning to Teach Subjects in the Secondary School Series

Edited by Susan Capel, Marilyn Leask and Tony Turner

Designed for all students learning to teach in the secondary school and particularly those on school-based initial teacher training courses, the books in this series complement our best-selling textbook *Learning to Teach in the Secondary School* and its companion *Starting to Teach in the Secondary School*.

Learning to Teach in the Secondary School
A Companion to School Experience   2nd Edition

Susan Capel, Marilyn Leask and Tony Turner

1999: 504pp
Pb: 0–415–19937–9: £16.99

The series also includes:

Learning to Teach Geography in the Secondary School
A Companion to School Experience

David Lambert and David Balderstone

2000: 516pp
Pb: 0–415–15676–9: £18.99

Learning to Teach Science in the Secondary School
A Companion to School Experience

Tony Turner and Wendy DiMarco

1998: 352pp
Pb: 0–415–15302–6: £16.50

Learning to Teach Design and Technology in the Secondary School
A Companion to School Experience

Gwyneth Owen-Jackson

2000: 184pp
Pb: 0–415–21693–1: £16.99

Learning to Teach RE in the Secondary School
A Companion to School Experience

Edited by Andrew Wright and Anne-Marie Brandom

2000: 336pp
Pb: 0–415–19436–9: £16.50

Learning to Teach Art and Design in the Secondary School
A Companion to School Experience

Edited by Nicholas Addison and Lesley Burgess

2000: 392pp
Pb: 0–415–16881–3: £16.99

Learning to Teach English in the Secondary School
A Companion to School Experience

Jon Davison and Jane Dowson

1997: 352pp
Pb: 0–415–15677–7: £16.50

Learning to Teach History in the Secondary School
A Companion to School Experience

Terry Hadyn, James Arthur and Martin Hunt

1997: 320pp
Pb: 0–415–15453–7: £16.50

Learning to Teach Mathematics in the Secondary School
A Companion to School Experience

Edited by Sue Johnston-Wilde, Peter Johnston-Wilde, David Pimm and John Westwell

1999: 288pp
Pb: 0–415–16280–7: £16.50

Learning to Teach ICT in the Secondary School

A Companion to School Experience

Edited by Marilyn Leask and Norbert Pachler

1999: 296pp
Pb: 0–415–19432–6: £16.50

Learning to Teach Modern Foreign Languages in the Secondary School

A Companion to School Experience

Norbert Pachler and Kit Field

1997: 416pp
Pb: 0–415–16281–5: £16.50

Learning to Teach Physical Education in the Secondary School

A Companion to School Experience

Susan Capel

1997: 368pp
Pb: 0–415–15301–8: £16.50

Starting to Teach in the Secondary School

A Companion for the Newly Qualified Teacher

Susan Capel, Marilyn Leask and Tony Turner

1996: 320pp
Pb: 0–415–13278–9: £16.50

All these books are available from your normal bookshop or supplier. If you require further information, or the RoutledgeFalmer catalogue, please call Huw Neill on +44 0207 842 2152, or look at our website on
www.routledgefalmer.com

Photocopiable Practical Resources for Secondary Schools

Classroom Behaviour Management Titles from RoutledgeFalmer

NEW

Educating Children with AD/HD
A Teacher's Manual

Paul Cooper and Fintan O'Regan

Attention Deficit/Hyperactivity Disorder (AD/HD) is the most common behavioural disorder affecting up to 5% of children in the UK. This book provides a concise and comprehensive guide to educating children with AD/HD. It offers a theoretical introduction to AD/HD and practical guidance to the classroom teacher on how to support children with this condition.

The book is rooted in the experience of practitioners who work on a daily basis with children with AD/HD, and draws upon up-to-date research evidence on the topic. The authors challenge crude assumptions about AD/HD and argue that the best way to understand AD/HD is as a condition in which biological and environmental factors interact. Suitable for use as a teaching manual and a training resource, *Educating Children with AD/HD* will help teachers, other educational workers and students develop a sense of empowerment in relation to AD/HD to teachers.

June 2001: 112pp
Pb: 0–415 21387–8: £25.00

Surviving and Succeeding in Difficult Classrooms
Paul Blum

Focusing on the secondary school, but of great value to classroom teachers everywhere, this book offers sensible, practical advice on what to do to survive and succeed in the face of troublesome classroom behaviour.

'**This is an excellent book in that it provides guidance to new teachers on the foundation of good classroom behaviour management and it is also recommended reading for staff tutors wishing to provide mentoring support for colleagues.**' – *School Leadership and Management*

'**This is a book for teachers ... nobody before has managed to convey the extent and degree of ill-discipline with such clarity.**' – Peter Kingston of the *Guardian*

1998: 160pp
Pb: 0–415–18523–8: £12.99

All these books are available from your normal bookshop or supplier. If you require further information, or the RoutledgeFalmer catalogue, please call Huw Neill on +44 0207 842 2152, or look at our website on www.routledgefalmer.com

Inclusive Education Books
from RoutledgeFalmer

Special Educational Needs in Schools

2nd Edition

Sally Beveridge

This new edition of Sally Beveridge's renowned work provides a concise but comprehensive overview of key issues in provision for children with special needs in schools, emphasising the role of the mainstream classroom teacher. This second edition looks at the numerous changes in special educational policy and practice that have taken place in the past five years. Topics covered include:

- Concepts of SEN
- The legislative framework
- The range of special educational need and provision
- Teaching approaches and organisational strategies
- Frameworks of support

1999: 160pp
Hb: 0–415–20293–0: £42.50
Pb: 0–415–20294–9: £13.99

Photocopiable Resource

The Special Educational Needs Co-ordinator's Handbook
A Guide for Implementing the Code of Practice

Garry Hornby, Gregan Davies and Geoff Taylor

'It offers clear guidelines through the assessment procedures and supplements them with helpful proformas and illustrative material ... all in all, it should enhance the educational provision offered to pupils with special needs by helping schools to implement the Code of Practice effectively.' – *Times Educational Supplement*

'Easy to read and well-organised. The *Handbook* will be a useful resource in responding to the Code and in stimulating solutions to the challenges.' – *Educational Research*

'This publication will provide concrete support in making action for SEN pupils a reality in your school.' – *Junior Education*

1995: A4: 192pp
Pb: 0–415–11683–X: £27.50

All these books are available from your normal bookshop or supplier. If you require further information, or the RoutledgeFalmer catalogue, please call Huw Neill on +44 0207 842 2152, or look at our website on www.routledgefalmer.com